RESEARCH BIBLIOGRAPHIES & CHECKLISTS

27

Michel Butor

RESEARCH BIBLIOGRAPHIES & CHECKLISTS

General editors

A. D. Deyermond, J. R. Little and J. E. Varey

MICHEL BUTOR

A CHECKLIST

by

Barbara Mason

Grant & Cutler Ltd

1979

ISBN 0 7293 0078 1

I.S.B.N. 84-499-3759-0

DEPÓSITO LEGAL: V. 1.215 - 1980

Printed in Spain by Artes Gráficas Soler, S.A., Valencia

for

GRANT & CUTLER LTD
11, BUCKINGHAM STREET, LONDON, W.C.2

CONTENTS

INTRODUCTION

The aim of the present volume is to provide students of Michel Butor's writings with a research tool. It is intended both to bring to their attention the numerous works written by Butor, particularly those published in rare and limited editions and to enable them to locate the mass of critical work already available on him. Two specific problems arise in compiling this bibliography. Firstly the bibliographer must take into account the vast amount of material which Butor has republished on different occasions, sometimes with significant textual changes, sometimes with illustrations, sometimes with altered typographical layout. Secondly he must indicate the scope of Butor's work, his preoccupation with collaboration and his interest in inter-disciplinary experiments. While this volume attempts to do both, it does not establish Butor's achievements by means of arbitrary classifications of writer, collaborator, critic, but instead presents the totality of his work. I have tried to make reference to material published before December 1977, but I have also included a small number of later items where these have been brought to my attention. I am aware that involuntary omissions will exist in a work of this nature and welcome any supplementary information from users of this volume.

The Bibliography is divided in the following way:

A: Primary material
    a: Books, including catalogues
    b: Articles, essays, critical essays, poems, notes, prefaces
    c: Interviews
    d: Translations by Butor
    e: English translations of a and b

B: Secondary material
    a: Books, periodicals and theses wholly or substantially devoted to Butor
    b: Articles, including less substantial parts of books, and references

Items are numbered in alphabetical order within each section.
However, the following observations need to be made:

Aa: Each edition of an item is numbered separately. Catalogues written by Butor for art exhibitions are included within this section, as are works which involve some degree of collaboration. Where Butor's texts are illustrated, this is indicated. The reader must be aware that it is misleading and against Butor's intentions to classify works in this way since they are the fruit of collaborative effort, but for the purposes of this volume, it is necessary to list them under a single author. Thus while the original text of *Litanie d'eau* (Aa37) comprises material jointly produced by Michel Butor and Gregory Masurovsky, it is listed with the rest of Butor's works and reference to Masurovsky's collaboration is made after the title. References to recordings and performances of certain works are also noted. Cross-references are made to Ab and within Aa where appropriate, and to reviews listed under Bb.

Ab: Articles are listed alphabetically. Butor's particular practice of rewriting and republishing works is taken into account so that where appropriate cross-reference is made to appearance in Aa and to different versions as well as to alternative titles. Lack of space however does not allow me to give details of the way in which works are revised or altered in each case. It is worth noting here that on occasions Butor's page numbers follow unusual sequences in order to create a sense of interlocking movement and textual mobility. An example of this is provided by Ab92. The volume of the Belgian review *L'VII* partly devoted to Butor is listed at the end (Ab281). It is impossible to classify this ambiguously titled review within the alphabetical system used. Debates or discussions in which Butor has participated are also included here.

Ac: Interviews are listed alphabetically by the surname of the person conducting the interview. One book, a series of interviews, is included in this section (Ac19) and a cross-reference is made to Ba.

Ad: Works translated by Butor are given in alphabetical order of the name of the author.

Ae: For practical reasons only translations into English have been included although work has been done in other languages, notably German and Spanish. The first part is devoted to books, the second to articles.

Ba: Alphabetical order by author, or, in the case of a special number of a periodical, by periodical title. By 'substantial' is meant one-third of a book or more. Included within this section is the special edition of *L'Arc* (Ba2). The classification of this item is but one example of the type of problems facing the bibliographer of Butor. Although it is not strictly a work written by Butor himself, he prescribed its collaborative nature and decided on its final format. He also contributed several articles to it. However it is placed here under secondary material since a large part of the review was written by people other than Butor himself. Once again this is a collaborative work bridging the gap between Aa, Ab and Ba. Its inclusion in this particular section is not without a degree of arbitrariness.

Bb: Articles are listed alphabetically by author, and within a given author alphabetically by title. Critical reviews ('CR') are listed after titled articles alphabetically and numerically according to the work reviewed. Anonymous articles and reviews are given at the end. Passing references to Butor are not included, nor are entries in encyclopædias.

In general, presentation needs little further explanation. Abbreviations are minimal and self-evident. Thus MB = Michel Butor, CR = critical review (or *compte rendu*), repr. = reprinted (or *repris*), n.p. = not paginated. An asterisk indicates that I have not seen the item in question.

I am particularly indebted to Michel Butor for his help and interest in the compilation of this volume. My gratitude also goes to the staff of the University Library, Lancaster, the Bibliothèque Nationale in Paris, and those connected with the *Fonds Michel Butor* at the Bibliothèque Municipale at Nice. I owe a further debt to the editor, Professor Roger Little, for his valuable advice and guidance. Finally my thanks go to Steven Donhowe for his unfailing patience and encouragement.

Lancaster, 1978   B.M.

A: PRIMARY MATERIAL

Aa BOOKS AND CATALOGUES

Aa1   *Avertissement aux locataires indésirables*, Larroque: Moulin Larroque, 1974, n.p., [18] pp.
Drawings by Ania Staritsky.

Aa2   *La Banlieue de l'aube à l'aurore. Mouvement brownien*, Montpellier: Fata Morgana, 1968, n.p.
Illustrations by Bernard Dufour. Contains Ab17, 138. CR: see Bb340.

Aa3   *Bryen en temps conjugués*, Paris: Galerie de Seine, 1975, 49pp.
Illustrations by Camille Bryen.

Aa4* *Carte commentée*, Veilhes: Puel, Coll. Le Bouquet, 1974, n.p., [22] pp.

Aa5   *Chacun son cadeau* (collaboration of T. Kitada), Paris: Hachette, Coll. Le Vert Paradis, 1977, 32pp.

Aa6   *Champ de vitres*, Paris: Galerie Weil, 1969.
Illustrations by Cesare Peverelli. Also in different form in Aa33. Also as Ab28.

Aa7   *Une Chanson pour Don Juan*, Veilhes: Puel, 1973, n.p., [25] pp.
Illustrations by Ania Staritsky and poster. Also in different form in Ab29.

Aa8* *Comme Shirley*, Paris: La Hune, 1966, n.p.
Illustrations by Gregory Masurovsky. Limited to 1000 copies. Also in different form in Aa31. Also in Aa52, pp.73-82. Also as Ab35.

Aa9   *Les Compagnons de Pantagruel* (Zaharoff Lecture), London: Oxford Univ. Press, 1976.

Aa10* *Conditionnement*, Montréal: Galerie Soixante, n.p.
Illustrations by Edmund Alleyn. Also in different form in Aa33. Also as Ab36.

Aa11* *Cycle, sur neuf gouaches d'Alexander Calder*, Paris: La Hune, 1962, 9pp.

Illustrations by Alexander Calder. Also in different form in Aa30. Also as Ab49.

Aa12 *Degrés*, Paris: Gallimard, 1960, 392pp.

CR: see Bb6, 73, 116, 118, 176, 205, 255, 282, 346, 369, 373, 384, 406, 434, 493, 560, 585, 653, 718.

Aa13 *Delvaux*, Lausanne, Paris: Bibliothèque des Arts, 1975, 325pp.

Collaboration of Jean Clair, Suzanne Houbart-Wilkin. Catalogue of paintings. 40 illus. in colour, 330 illus. in black and white. Also as Ab225.

Aa14 *Description de San Marco*, Paris: Gallimard, 1963, 111pp., fold plan.

Contains Ab2, 18, 183, 269, 270, 271. CR: see Bb114, 135, 156, 283, 301, 451, 476.

Aa15* *Devises fantômes*, Paris: C. Martinez, 1976, n.p., [27]pp.

Illustrations by Ania Staritsky. Cover illus.

Aa16 *Dialogue avec 33 variations de Ludwig van Beethoven sur une valse de Diabelli*, Paris: Gallimard, Coll. Le Chemin, 1971, 160pp.

CR: see Bb94, 150, 296, 323, 444, 477, 624, 719.

Aa17 *Dialogue des règnes*, Paris: Brunidor, 1967, n.p.

Also in different form in Aa31, 59, 84. Also as Ab54. CR: see Bb12.

Aa18* ——, Paris: Castella, 1968, n.p.

Water-colours by Jacques Hérold. Limited to 100 copies. 75 copies numbered from 1-75 and 20 numbered from I to XX. Signed by MB and Jacques Hérold.

Aa19* *Eclats*, Paris: Lucien Weil, 1970.

Also in different form in Aa33.

Aa20 *L'Emploi du temps*, Paris: Editions de Minuit, 1956, 304pp.

CR: see Bb22, 44, 128, 244, 252, 256, 276, 313, 370, 396, 407, 410, 465, 486, 580, 586, 644, 654, 659.

Aa21 ——, Paris: Union Générale d'Editions, Coll. 10/18, no. 305, 1966, 512pp.

Bb513 as postface. CR: see Bb168.

Aa22 *Essais sur le roman*, Paris: Gallimard, Coll. Idées, 188, 1969, 184pp.

Selections reprinted from Aa67 and Aa68. Contains Ab47, 62, 69, 89,

94, 115, 118, 180, 208, 232, 235, 248, 265. CR: see Bb131.

Aa23 *Essais sur les 'Essais'*, Paris: Gallimard, Coll. Les Essais, 1968, 216pp.
Contains Ab159. CR: see Bb7, 119, 303, 324, 720.

Aa24 *Essais sur les modernes*, Paris: Gallimard, Coll. Idées, 61, 1964, 376pp.
Selections reprinted from Aa67 and Aa68. Contains Aa54; Ab12, 45, 70, 107, 121, 132, 152, 165, 177, 188, 211, 252, 256.

Aa25 *Le Génie du lieu*, Paris: Bernard Grasset, 1958, 209pp.
Contains Ab43, 52, 63, 76, 97, 122, 123, 238. CR: see Bb14, 314, 366, 371, 471, 484, 634.

Aa26 *Hérold*, Paris: Galerie la Cour d'Ingres, 1959, 26pp. illus.

Aa27 *Hérold. Essai sur la peinture*, Paris: Editions Georges Fall, Coll. Musée de Poche, 1964, 82pp. 57pls.

Aa28 *Histoire extraordinaire, essai sur un rêve de Baudelaire*, Paris: Gallimard, 1961, 272pp.
CR: see Bb63, 84, 111, 117, 144, 169, 191, 206, 304, 385, 398, 429.

Aa29 *Hoirie voirie*, Turin: Olivetti, 1970.
Illustrations by Pierre Alechinsky. Also in different form in Aa33. Also as Ab86.

Aa30 *Illustrations*, Paris: Gallimard, Coll. Le Chemin, 1964, 216pp.
Contains Aa11, 37, 66; Ab4, 26, 38, 49, 79, 114, 213. CR: see Bb140, 261, 721.

Aa31 *Illustrations II*, Paris: Gallimard, Coll. Le Chemin, 1969, 271pp.
Contains Aa8, 17, 34, 80; Ab35, 50, 54, 92, 154, 170, 186, 210, 244. CR: see Bb74, 469, 523, 722.

Aa32 *Illustrations III*, Paris: Gallimard, Coll. Le Chemin, 1973, 155pp.
Contains Aa36, 50, 60; Ab44, 112, 128, 130, 178, 201, 212. CR: see Bb67, 75, 182, 297, 305, 723.

Aa33 *Illustrations IV*, Paris: Gallimard, Coll. Le Chemin, 1974, 144pp.
Contains Aa6, 10, 19, 29, 53, 62, 83, 90; Ab28, 36, 60, 68, 86, 147, 149, 167, 176, 189, 259, 264, 278. CR: see Bb137, 514, 546.

Aa34 *Les Incertitudes de Psyché*, Paris: Le Club Français du Livre, 1964.
Lithograph by André Masson. Also in different form in Aa31. Also as Ab92.

Aa35 *Intervalle. Anecdote en expansion*, Paris: Gallimard, Coll. Le Chemin, 1973, 161pp.

L'Enchantement created from *Intervalle* by MB and Robert Mazoyer and shown on French television, 6.2.1974. CR: see Bb67, 75, 159, 175, 182, 297, 305, 575, 723.

Aa36 *Lettres écrites du Nouveau Mexique en réponse à quatre gravures de Camille Bryen*, Paris: Brunidor, 1970, n.p., [19]pp.

Illustrations in colour by Camille Bryen. Also in different form in Aa32. Also as Ab201.

Aa37 *Litanie d'eau*, Paris: La Hune, 1964, n.p.

10 original drawings by Gregory Masurovsky. Table of contents is full-page water-colour of the 10 drawings in miniature. Limited to 105 copies signed by MB and Gregory Masurovsky. Also in different form in Aa30. Also in Aa52, pp.19-52. Also as Ab114.

Aa38* *Le Livre et l'artiste*, Paris, 1976 (catalogue).

Aa39* *Maccheroni, Henri* (collaboration of Jean-Louis Roure and Roger Galizot), Paris: Musée d'Art Moderne, 1975 (catalogue).

Aa40 *Matière de rêves*, Paris: Gallimard, 1975, 136pp.

Contains Aa72; Ab218, 221, 222, 226, 229. CR: see Bb37, 68, 138, 284, 325, 515, 530.

Aa41 *Mobile, étude pour une représentation des Etats-Unis*, Paris: Gallimard, 1962, 333pp.

CR: see Bb21, 46, 60, 76, 92, 107, 133, 184, 306, 450, 587, 655, 724, 725, 726.

Aa42 *La Modification*, Paris: Editions de Minuit, 1957, 236pp.

CR: see Bb23, 24, 36, 41, 50, 61, 105, 109, 113, 120, 162, 216, 229, 232, 251, 257, 265, 269, 272, 315, 358, 372, 386, 411, 413, 425, 452, 483, 487, 520, 536, 561, 562, 597, 681.
[*La Modification*, film based on MB's novel, adapted for screen by Raphael Cluzet and Michel Worms. Director: Michel Worms, Paris: Serge Vincent-Vital, Œdipe films, 237pp. scenario.]

Aa43 —, Ottawa: Le Cercle du Livre de France, 1958, 267pp.

Aa44 —, Paris: Le Club Français du Livre, 1959, 304pp.

Aa45 —, Paris: Union Générale d'Editions, Coll. 10/18, 1962, 312pp. Bb357 as postface.

Aa46 —, Lausanne: La Guilde du Livre, 1965, 228pp.

Aa47 —, Paris: Rombaldi, 1970, 253pp.

Aa48 —, presented by Jacques Guicharnaud, Waltham, Mass: Ginn, French Literature Series, 1970, xxvii-284pp.

Aa49 —, ed. John Sturrock, London: Methuen, Methuen's Twentieth Century Texts, 1971, xxvii-259pp. Bb619 as introduction.

Aa50* *Mon cher Marc-Jean*, Paris: Visat, 1965, n.p., [27] pp.
Drawings by Marc-Jean Masurovsky. Limited to 60 copies signed by author and artist. Also in Aa32, p.9; also in Aa52, pp.53-60; also as part of Ab44.

Aa51 *Les Mots dans la peinture*, Geneva: Albert Skira, Coll. Les Sentiers de la Création, 1969, 182pp. illus.; also in Aa70, pp.31-95.
Also as Ab137. CR: see Bb221, 326, 351, 478, 722.

Aa52 *Obliques*, special issue devoted to MB and Gregory Masurovsky, 1975, 160pp.
Contains Aa8, 37, 50, 53, 59 (frontispiece), 61 (extracts), 90; Ab33, 82, 96, 114, 136, 139, 146, 172, 230, 236, 267, 277; Bb509.

Aa53 *L'Oeil des Sargasses*, Sint Pieters Kapelle (Belgium): Lettera Amorosa, 1972, n.p.
Original frontispiece by Gregory Masurovsky. Also in different form in Aa33. Also in Aa52, pp.86-102.

Aa54 *Les Oeuvres d'art imaginaires chez Proust*, (Cassal Bequest Lecture) London: Athlone Press, 1964, 45pp.
Also in Aa24; also in Aa68. CR: see Bb727.

Aa55* *L'Oreille de la lune. Voyage en compagnie de Jules Verne*, Boulogne-sur-Seine: R. Blanchet, 1973, 40pp.
In folio de luxe edition with illustrations by Robert Blanchet. Limited to 200 copies. Signed by author in pencil.

Aa56 *Où, le génie du lieu, 2*, Paris: Gallimard, 1971, 400pp.
Contains Ab22, 23, 78, 100, 103, 142, 143, 261. CR: see Bb150, 296, 327, 408, 444, 477, 719.

Aa57 *Passage de Milan*, Paris: Editions de Minuit, 1954, 286pp.
CR: see Bb110, 128, 163, 292, 307, 400, 466, 589.

Aa58 —, Paris: U.G.E., Coll. 10/18, 505, 1970, 265pp.

Aa59 *Paysage de répons suivi de Dialogue des règnes*, Albeuve: Editions Castella, 1968, 61pp.
Contains in different form Aa17, 31, 84 (extracts); Ab54, 170 (extracts), 171. Frontispiece repr. in Aa52, p.83. CR: see Bb164, 340.

Aa60   *Petites Liturgies pour hâter l'avènement du 'Grand transparent' de Jacques Hérold*, Paris: Galerie la Seine, 1972, 42pp.
Illustrations by Jacques Hérold. Also in different form in Aa32. Also as Ab178.

Aa61   *Les Petits Miroirs*, Paris: La Farandole, 1972, n.p., [19]pp.
Illustrations by Gregory Masurovsky. Extract in Aa52, pp.150-3.

Aa62   *La Politique des charmeuses*, Paris: Brunidor, 1969.
Illustrations by Jacques Hérold. Text printed on silk. Also in different form as Aa33. Also as Ab189.

Aa63   *Portrait de l'artiste en jeune singe, capriccio*, Paris: Gallimard, 1967, 237pp.
CR: see Bb8, 15, 77, 211, 285, 293, 308, 344, 360, 409, 419, 432, 446, 485, 640, 728, 729.

Aa64   *Querelle des états. Petit monument pour Charles Perrault, cinq triptyques ou contes de fées en poudre*, Paris: Brunidor, 1973.
Water-colours by Camille Bryen.

Aa65   *Rabelais ou c'était pour rire*, Paris: Larousse, Thèmes et Textes, 1972, 143pp.
Written with Denis Hollier. CR: see Bb529.

Aa66   *Rencontre*, Paris: Editions Galerie du Dragon, n.p.
Illustrated by Enrique Zañartu. Limited to 50 copies. Also in different form in Aa30. Also as Ab213.

Aa67   *Répertoire, études et conférences, 1948-1959*, Paris: Editions de Minuit, 1959, 274pp.
Contains Ab1, 12, 14, 16, 45, 62, 70, 107, 132, 165, 177, 188, 190, 205, 211, 215, 232, 251, 252, 253, 256. Parts reprinted in Aa22 and Aa24. CR: see Bb20, 235, 255, 345, 373, 434, 472, 560, 577, 706.

Aa68   *Répertoire II, études et conférences, 1959-1963*, Paris: Editions de Minuit, 1964, 301pp.
Contains Aa54; Ab13, 31, 47, 69, 89, 94, 115, 118, 121, 140, 145, 152, 168, 180, 204, 208, 235, 248, 249, 265, 273. Parts reprinted in Aa22 and Aa24. CR: see Bb170, 207, 212, 286, 294, 309, 397, 516, 588, 598, 656, 730.

Aa69   *Répertoire III*, Paris: Editions de Minuit, Coll. Critique, 1968, 407pp., 21pls.
Contains Ab25, 32, 42, 46, 55, 83, 88, 111, 116, 134, 135, 155, 169, 241, 242, 246, 247, 255, 257, 262, 272. CR: see Bb87, 119, 328, 660, 720.

Aa70   *Répertoire IV*, Paris: Editions de Minuit, Coll. Critique, 1974, 447pp., 20pls.
Contains Aa51, 78; Ab10, 11, 30, 64, 66, 74, 85, 110, 127, 131, 137, 157, 164, 191, 199, 200, 240, 245, 250, 260, 276. CR: see Bb461, 479, 731.

Aa71   *Réseau aérien. Texte radiophonique*, Paris: Gallimard, 1962, 120pp.
Contains Ab160. CR: see Bb287. Broadcast by Radiodiffusion française, 16 June 1962.

Aa72   *Le Rêve de l'ammonite*, Montpellier: Fata Morgana, 1975.
Water-colours and lithographs by MB and Pierre Alechinsky. Also in different form in Aa40; also as Ab218.

Aa73   *Le Rêve de l'ombre*, Paris: Nouveau Cercle du Livre, 1976.
Water-colours by Cesare Peverelli. Also in different form in Aa76; also as Ab224.

Aa74*   *Revue rêvée*, Sint Pieters Kapelle (Belgium): Lettera Amorosa, 1977.

Aa75   *La Rose des vents. 32 rhumbs pour Charles Fourier*, Paris: Gallimard, Coll. Le Chemin, 1970, 172pp.
CR: see Bb9, 71, 298, 329, 722.

Aa76   *Second sous-sol. Matière de rêves II*, Paris: Gallimard, Coll. Le Chemin, 1976, 218pp.
Contains Aa73; Ab220, 223, 224, 225, 227. CR: see Bb139, 151, 220.

Aa77*   *Seigle*, Paris: Galerie Charpentier, 1963 (catalogue).

Aa78   *Les Sept Femmes de Gilbert le mauvais, autre heptaèdre*, Montpellier: Fata Morgana, Coll. Scholies, 1972.
Illustrations by Cesare Peverelli. Also in different form in Aa70. Also as Ab240.

Aa79   *6 810 000 litres d'eau par seconde, étude stéréophonique*, Paris: Gallimard, 1965, 281pp.
CR: see Bb78, 101, 157, 171, 173, 213, 278, 310, 347, 361, 417, 554, 732.

Aa80*   *Spirale*, Brussels: Palais des Beaux-Arts, 18pp.
Also in different form in Aa31. Also as Ab244.

Aa81*   *Strand, Paul* (collaboration with Jean-Claude Lemagny), Paris: Centre National d'Art et de Culture Georges Pompidou, 1977.

Aa82* *Le Test du titre*, Paris: Editions Losfeld, 1967.
Illustrations by Pierre Alechinsky.

Aa83 *Tourmente*, Montpellier: Fata Morgana, 1968.
Drawings by Pierre Alechinsky, Bernard Dufour and Jacques Hérold. In folder and limited to 130 copies. Also in different form in Aa33.

Aa84 *Travaux d'approche. Eocène, miocène, piocène*, Paris: Gallimard, Coll. Poésie, no. 84, 1972, 189pp.
Contains Aa59; Ab21, 54, 84, 170, 171, 175, 185; Ac6. CR: see Bb152, 330, 341, 480.

Aa85 ——, Paris: Brunidor, 1972.
Contains one illustration by Jacques Hérold.

Aa86 *Trio pour Jacques Hérold*, Fondation Royaumont, 1972 (catalogue).

Aa87 *Troisième dessous. Matière de rêves III*, Paris: Gallimard, Coll. Le Chemin, 1977, 256pp.

Aa88 *U.S.A. 76: bicentenaire kit*, Paris: Le Club du Livre, 1976, 96pp., 50 objects.
'Serigraphies de Jacques Monory et objets authentiques, modifiés, reproduits, parfois imaginés, glanés dans les cinquante États de l'Union, répertoriés . . . pour un bicentenaire et à l'occasion du deux centième anniversaire de la Déclaration d'indépendance, le 4 juillet 1976; édité par Philippe Lebaud.' Issued in blue box. Contains Ab57.

Aa89 *Votre Faust, fantaisie variable, genre opéra*, Paris: Gallimard, 1962, 90pp.
Also as three stereophonic records (no. 01 21580-6) with instruction book, set of playing cards, etc., Freiburg: Harmonia Mundi, 1973. Musical performance under title 'Portail de Votre Faust' in Brussels, Dec. 1966. World première of opera at La Piccola Scala, Milan, 15 Jan. 1969. Also as Ab275. CR: see Bb82, 102, 190, 299, 555.

Aa90 *Western Duo*, Los Angeles: Tamarind Lithography Workshop, 1969.
Collaboration of Gregory Masurovsky. Also in Aa33. Also in Aa52, pp.103-12. Also as Ab278.

Aa91 *Zañartu*, Paris: Editions Galerie du Dragon, 1958, 10pp. (catalogue).

Ab1   'L'Alchimie et son langage', *Critique*, IX, 77 (Oct. 53), 884-91; also in Aa67, pp.12-19.

Ab2   'A l'intérieur de Saint-Marc', *La Nouvelle Revue Française*, 127 (July 63), 76-85; 128 (Aug. 63), 285-90; 129 (Sept. 63), 465-71; also in Aa14.

'L'Aménagement du ciel', see Ab21.

Ab3   'A Paris' (with photographs by Inge Morath and Claude Michaelides), *L'Oeil*, 54 (June 59), 34-43.

Ab4   'L'Appel des Rocheuses' (with photographs by Ansel Adams and Edward Weston), *Réalités*, 197 (June 62), 76-83; also without photographs under title 'Les Montagnes Rocheuses' in Aa30, pp.91-105.

Ab5   'A propos de *L'Aventure de l'archéologie* de Ceram', *Arts*, 711 (25.2.59), 1-2, 4.

Ab6   'A quoi servez-vous? (Réponse de MB)', *La Nouvelle Critique*, 120 (Nov. 60), 12-13.

Ab7   'Archipel Shopping 1', *L'Arc*, 68 (1977), 89-96.

Ab8   'L'Art contemporain jugé par ses sources', *Les Lettres Nouvelles*, 11 (Feb. 61), 124-39.

Ab9   '*L'Attente l'oubli* de Maurice Blanchot', *Le Monde*, 5409 (9.6.62), 15.

'Au feu des pages', see Ab66.

Ab10   'Au gouffre du modèle', *XXe Siècle*, 19 (June 62), 89-92; also in Aa70, pp. 365-70.

Ab11   'Au moindre signe', *Mercure de France*, CXXI (Apr. 65), 594-609; also in Aa70, pp.351-64; also as preface to Per Olof Sundman, *L'Expédition* (tr. Chantal Chadenson), Paris: Gallimard, 1965.

Ab12   'Une Autobiographie dialectique', *Critique*, XI, 103 (Dec. 55), 1046-55; also in Aa24, pp.361-76; also in Aa67, pp.262-70.

'Aveux', see Ab191.

Ab13   'Babel en creux', *La Nouvelle Revue Française*, 112 (Apr. 62), 681-8; 113 (May 62), 876-85; also in Aa68, pp.199-214;

also as preface to Victor Hugo, *Œuvres complètes*, VIII, Paris: Le Club Français du Livre, 1968, pp.xix-xxxii.

Ab14 'La Balance des fées', *Les Cahiers du Sud*, XLI, 324 (Aug. 54), 183-95; also in Aa67, pp.61-73.

Ab15 'Balzac commence sa vraie carrière', *Arts*, 745 (21.10.59), 5.

Ab16 'Balzac et la réalité', *La Nouvelle Revue Française*, 80 (Aug. 59), 228-47; also in Aa67, pp.79-93.

Ab17 'La Banlieue de l'aube à l'aurore', in Aa2; also in Ab281, pp.45-66.

Ab18 'Le Baptistère de Saint-Marc', *L'Express*, 648 (14.11.63); also in Aa14.

Ab19 'Berlin', *Le Figaro Littéraire*, 845 (27.6.62), 1, 13.

Ab20 'Bienvenue à Duke Ellington, maître du raffinement et de l'ironie', *Arts*, 694 (29.10.58), 1, 9.

'Des *Bijoux indiscrets* à *L'Encyclopédie*', see Ab55.

Ab21 'Blues des projets', in Aa84, pp.133-85.
Contains the following extracts from Ba2: 'L'Aménagement du ciel', p.43; 'Conrad Witz', p.43; 'Franz Kline', p.59; 'Livres imaginaires', p.86; 'Les Machines imaginaires', p.5; 'Les Œuvres d'art imaginaires', p.43; 'Spectacles imaginaires', p.67; 'Suggestions', pp.19, 41, 59, 85, 99; 'La Vendeuse des Galeries Lafayette', p.5; 'Les Villes imaginaires', p.23.

'La Boue à Séoul', see Ab22.

Ab22* 'La Boue à Séoul; la pluie à Angkor', *Les Cahiers du Chemin*, 2 (15.1.68), 47-58; also in different form in Aa56, pp.21-38 and pp.41-66.

Ab23 'La Brume à Santa Barbara', in Aa56, pp.73-100.

Ab24 'Carlo Emilio Gadda', *L'Express*, XI, 621 (9.5.63), 33.

Ab25 'Le Carré et son habitant', *La Nouvelle Revue Française*, IX, 97 (Jan. 61), 119-27; 98 (Feb. 61), 315-27; also in Aa69, pp.307-24.

Ab26 'La Cathédrale de Laon: l'automne' (with photographs by Gilles Ehrmann), *Réalités*, 218 (Mar. 64), 33-9; also without photographs in Aa30, pp.189-99.

Ab27 *'Celui qui ne m'accompagnait pas* par Maurice Blanchot', *La Nouvelle Nouvelle Revue Française*, 8 (Aug. 53), 331-2.

'Ce que dit *La Femme 100 têtes*', see Ab127.

Ab28 'Champ de vitres pour Cesare Peverelli', *La Nouvelle Revue Française*, 212 (Aug. 70), 21-2; also in Aa33, pp. 130-7. Originally published as Aa6.

Ab29* 'Une Chanson pour Don Juan', *Degrés*, 1 (Jan. 73), 1- 10; also in *Alif* (Tunis), 3 (Nov. 73), 30-2; also in Aa7.

Ab30 'Charles Fourier', *Les Cahiers du Chemin*, 16 (15.10.71), 58-73; also as preface to Charles Fourier, *Le Nouveau Monde industriel et sociétaire*, Paris: Flammarion, 1973; also under title 'Le Féminin chez Fourier', in Aa70, pp.193-207.

Ab31 'Chateaubriand et l'ancienne Amérique', *La Nouvelle Revue Française*, 132 (Dec. 63), 1015-31; 133 (Jan. 64), 63-77; 134 (Feb. 64), 230-50; also in Aa68, pp.152-92.

Ab32 'Claude Monet ou le monde renversé', *Art de France*, 3 (15.12.62), 277-300; also in Aa69, pp.241-58.

Ab33 'Clefs des approches', in Aa52, p.120.

Ab34 'Comment se sont écrits certains de mes livres', in *Nouveau Roman, hier aujourd'hui, 2*, ed. Jean Ricardou, Paris: Union Générale d'Editions, 1972, pp.243-54; extract in *Magazine Littéraire*, 71 (Dec. 72), 54-6.

Ab35 'Comme Shirley', in Aa31, pp.38-224. Originally published as Aa8.

Ab36* 'Conditionnement', *Opus International*, 3 (Oct. 69), 39-43; also in different form in Aa33, pp. 16-46; also as Aa10.

'Conrad Witz', see Ab21.

Ab37 'Considérez-vous que l'intelligence traverse actuellement une crise?', *Arts*, 892 (23.11.62), 18.

Ab38* 'La Conversation', *Les Cahiers des Saisons*, 9 (Feb.-Mar. 57), 199-203; also in *Cyanur*, 15 (17.8.64), 3-9; also in Aa30, pp.9-29.

Ab39 'Conversation dans l'atelier: Bernard Dufour', *L'Oeil*, 100 (Apr. 63), 34-41.

Ab40* 'Conversation dans l'atelier: Paul Jenkins', *Cimaise*, 65 (July-Oct. 63), 14-16.

Ab41 'Conversation dans l'atelier: Bernard Saby', *L'Oeil*, 79-80 (July-Aug. 61), 36-43; also in *Bernard Saby*, Paris: L'Oeil, galerie d'art (12 Feb.-12 Mar.) (1963), n.p.

Ab42 'La Corbeille de l'Ambrosienne', *La Nouvelle Revue Française*, XIV, 84 (Dec. 59), 969-89; also in Aa69, pp.43-58.

Ab43 'Cordoue', in Aa25, pp.9-26; extract under title 'Cordoue' in *Les Lettres Nouvelles*, 36 (Mar. 56), 331-9.

Ab44 'Courrier d'images', in Aa32, pp.9, 46, 71, 82, 93, 117-18, 154-5. Aa50 (extract). Contains Ab112.

Ab45 'La Crise de croissance de la science-fiction', *Les Cahiers du Sud*, XLVI, 317 (Jan. 53), 31-9; also in Aa24, pp.223-37 and Aa67, pp.186-94.

Ab46 'La Critique et l'invention', *Critique*, XXIII, 247 (Dec. 67), 984-95; also in Aa69, pp.7-20.

Ab47 'Le Critique et son public' in Aa22, pp.162-72; also in Aa68, pp.127-34. Extracts under title 'L'Ecrivain et son public' in *Les Lettres Françaises*, 1016 (13.2.64), 8.

Ab48 'Culture' (with **MB**, Georges Borgeaud, Michel Carrouges *et al*), *La Vie Intellectuelle*, 6 (June 48), 32-64.

Ab49 'Cycle', *Les Lettres Françaises*, 931 (14.6.62), 5; also in Aa30, pp.79-89; also as Aa11.

Ab50 'Dans les flammes: chanson du moine à madame Nhu', *Tel Quel*, 24 (Wint. 66), 24-39; also in Aa31, pp.10-77, 14-33, 17-31, 50-68; also in German in *In den Flammen* (watercolours by Ruth Francken), Stuttgart: Belser, 1966.*

Ab51 'Le Début d'un voyage', *Le Monde*, 9351 (7.2.75), 20.

Ab52 'Delphes', in Aa25, pp.59-87; extract 'Delphes' in *Les Lettres Nouvelles*, 45 (Jan. 57), 38-51.

Ab53 'Dialogue à propos de "Un printemps à New York" ', *Les Lettres Françaises*, 1285 (28.5.69), 3, 4, 5, 12.

Ab54 'Dialogues des règnes', *La Nouvelle Revue Française*, 173 (May 67), 983-96; also in Aa31, pp.40-157, 46-73, 51-69, 86-100, 112-46; also in Aa17; also in Aa59; also in Aa84 in different form and combined with 'Paysage de répons'.

Ab55 'Diderot le fataliste et ses maîtres', *Critique*, XXII, 228 (May 66), 387-418; 230 (July 66), 619-41; also in Aa69, pp.103-58; also under title 'Des *Bijoux indiscrets* à *L'Encyclopédie*', in Denis Diderot, *Œuvres complètes*, Paris: Le Club Français du Livre, 1969.

Ab56* 'Diorama pour le muséum. 1948', *Shi'r* (Beirut), 18 (Spr. 61).

Ab57 '18 blues pour Jacques Monory', *Les Cahiers du Chemin*, 23 (15.10.75), 54-60; also as part of Aa88.

Ab58* 'Don Juan dans l'Essonne', *Métamorphoses*, 19-20 (Wint. 72-3), 136-41.

Ab59 'Don Juan dans les Yvelines', *Obliques*, 4 (1973), 2-16, 27-62, 135-46.

Ab60 'Eclats', in Aa33, pp.132-3; also as Aa19.

Ab61 'Ecorché vif', in Ba21, pp.435-42 (followed by a discussion, pp.443-50).

Ab62 'L'Ecriture pour moi est une colonne vertébrale', *Les Nouvelles Littéraires*, 1640 (5.2.59), 7; also under title 'Intervention à Royaumont', in Aa22, pp.15-20; also in Aa67, pp.271-4.

'L'Ecrivain et son public', see Ab47.

Ab63 'Egypte', in Aa25, pp.109-210. Extracts under title 'Le Paysage de la vallée', *La Nouvelle Nouvelle Revue Française*, 64 (Apr. 58), 594-609, and 'Le Printemps en Haute-Egypte', *France-Observateur*, 409 (13.3.58), 13-14, and 'Louqsor', *Les Lettres Nouvelles*, 59 (Apr. 58), 487-97.

Ab64 'Eloge de la machine-à-écrire', *L'Arc*, 50 (1972), 6-8; also in Aa70, pp.425-9.

Ab65 '*L'Elu* de Thomas Mann', *Monde Nouveau Paru*, 62 (1952), 80-1.

Ab66 'Emile Zola romancier expérimental et la flamme bleue', *Critique*, XXIII, 239 (Apr. 67), 407-37; also in Aa70, pp.259-91. Extracts under title 'Au feu des pages', *Cahiers Naturalistes*, 34 (1967), 101-13 and *Les Lettres Françaises*, 1215 (3.1.68), 12-14, and 'Zola et l'expérimentation romanesque', *La Quinzaine Littéraire*, 24 (15.3.67), 10-11. CR: see Bb650.

Ab67 'Entre *Les Mille et une nuits* et *Barbe-Bleue*', *Le Monde*, 8237 (9.7.71), 15.

Ab68 'Epître à Georges Perros', in Aa33, pp.24-9.

Ab69 'L'Espace du roman', in Aa22, pp.48-58; also in Aa68, pp.42-50. Extraits in *Les Nouvelles Littéraires*, 1753 (6.4.61), and in *Revue d'Esthétique* (Paris), XV (Jan.-Mar. 62), 91-7.

Ab70 'Esquisse d'un seuil pour Finnegan', *La Nouvelle Nouvelle Revue Française*, 60 (Dec. 57), 1033-53; also in Aa24, pp.283-309; also in Aa67, pp.219-33; also as introduction to James Joyce, *Finnegans Wake* (fragments adapted by A. du Bouchet), Paris: Gallimard, 1962.

Ab71   'Les Européens et les Bostoniennes', *Monde Nouveau*, 94 (Nov. 55), 136-9.

Ab72   'Excuse en orbite', *L'Arc*, 64 (1976), [89-90].

'La Faim et la soif', see Ab85.

Ab73   'Fantaisie chromatique à propos de Stendhal', *Les Cahiers du Chemin*, 21 (15.4.74), 86-114.

Ab74   'La Fascinatrice', *Les Cahiers du Chemin*, 4 (15.10.68), 20-55; also in Aa70, pp.371-97.

'Le Féminin chez Fourier', see Ab30.

Ab75   'Femmes terribles: Athalie', *Mercure de France*, 1172 (Apr. 61), 669-71.

Ab76   'Ferrare', in Aa25, pp.101-5.

Ab77   'Flic flac', *Le Monde*, 7272 (1.6.68), 11.
Illustration of poster in Aa70 opposite p.320.

'La Forme de la tentation', see Ab245.

'Franz Kline', see Ab21.

Ab78   'Le Froid à Zuni', in Aa56, pp.217-388.

'La Gare Saint-Lazare', see Ab79.

Ab79   'Gare Saint-Lazare, lève-toi et marche!' (with photographs by J. P. Charbonnier), *Réalités*, 182 (Mar. 61), 50-9; also without photographs under title 'La Gare Saint-Lazare', in Aa30, pp.55-77.

'Germe d'encre', see Ab272.

Ab80   'Grandeur et servitude littéraires', *Education*, 143 (18.6.72), 24-7.

Ab81   'Grand prix 53 de la photo aux U.S.A.-Henri Cartier-Bresson sous l'objectif de MB', *Arts*, 699 (3.12.58), 5.

Ab82   'Grille', in Aa52, pp.122-3.

Ab83   'Heptaèdre héliotrope', *La Nouvelle Revue Française*, 173 (Apr. 67), 750-79; also in Aa69, pp.325-50.

Ab84* 'Hespérides et harengs', in Aa84, pp.41-71; extracts under title 'Hespérides' in *L'VII* (Brussels), 13-14 (Apr.-May 63), 105-15 and *Les Cahiers des Saisons*, 18 (Aut. 59).

Ab85 'Les Hiéroglyphes et les dés', in Aa70, pp. 121-91.

Contains 'La Faim et la soif', *Critique*, XXIV, 257 (Oct. 68), 827-54; 'Le Parler populaire et les langues anciennes', *Cahiers de la Compagnie Madeleine Renaud-Jean-Louis Barrault*, 67 (Sept. 68); 'Rabelais et les hiéroglyphes', *Saggi e Ricerche di Letteratura Francese*, IX (1968); '6/7 ou les dés de Rabelais', *Littérature*, 2 (May 71); also as preface to François Rabelais, *Le Cinquième Livre suivi d'œuvres diverses* (ed. P. Michel), Paris: Gallimard, 1969.

Ab86 'Hoirie voirie', in Aa33, pp.80-104; also as Aa29.

'Hokusaï', see Ab262.

'Hokusaï II', see Ab262.

Ab87 * 'Hommage partiel à Max Ernst', *Vrille* (25.7.45), n.p.

'L'Hospitalité de Mallia', see Ab122.

Ab88 'L'Ile au bout du monde', *La Nouvelle Revue Française*, 160 (Apr. 66), 620-36; 161 (May 66), 808-20; 162 (June 66), 1007-23; also in Aa69, pp.59-101.

Ab89 'Il peut y avoir une physique du livre', *Le Figaro Littéraire*, 835 (21.4.62), 1, 7; also in Aa22, pp.100-4; also under title 'Sur la page' in Aa68, pp.125-9.

Ab90 'L'Image du monde au 19e siècle', *Arts et Loisirs*, 27 (30.3. 66), 9-10.

Ab91* 'Imaginez', preface to *Poème électronique de Le Corbusier*, Paris: Editions de Minuit, 1958.

Ab92 'Les Incertitudes de Psyché', in Aa31, pp.104-223, 108-51, 113-47, 161-75, 196-216; also as Aa34; also extract in *La Nouvelle Revue Française*, 192 (Dec. 68), 732-5.

Ab93 'D'Incomparables Fantômes', *Le Figaro Littéraire*, 891 (18.5. 63), 15.

Ab94 'Individu et groupe dans le roman', *Les Cahiers du Sud*, XLIX, 365 (Feb.-Mar. 62), 79-109; also in *Cahiers de L'Association des Etudes Françaises*, 14 (Mar. 62), 115-31; also in Aa22, pp.89-108; also in Aa68, pp.73-87.

Ab95 'Influence des formes musicales sur quelques œuvres', *Musique en Jeu*, 4 (Oct. 71), 63-72.

'L'Inscription dans le portrait', see Ab137.

Ab96 'Intersection', in Aa52, p.134.

'Intervention à Royaumont', see Ab62.

Ab97 'Istanbul', *Monde Nouveau*, 92 (Sept. 55), 118-23; also in Aa25, pp.29-40.

Ab98* 'Itinéraires parisiens', *L'Oeil* (July 58).

Ab99 'Jacques Hérold', *Pour l'Art*, 69 (1959), 26-8.

Ab100 'J'ai fui Paris', in Aa56, pp.7-14, 385-92.

Ab101 'Jalons', *La Nouvelle Revue Française*, 212 (Aug. 70), 17-18.

Ab102 *'Jean Santeuil* par Marcel Proust', *Monde Nouveau Paru*, 62 (1952), 73-5.

Ab103 'Je hais Paris', *Les Cahiers du Chemin*, 7 (15.10.69), 103-18; also in Aa56, pp.103-44.

Ab104* 'Je n'y arriverai pas', *Plus*, 3 (Wint. 1959-60), 16 [dated 1948].

Ab105 'Des Jeunes Gens de mauvais goût', *Les Lettres Françaises*, 856 (29.12.60), 1.

Ab106 'Les Jeunes Romanciers ne sont pas mûrs pour le théâtre', *Arts*, 729 (1.7.59), 5.

Ab107 *'Le Joueur'*, preface to Dostoïevski, *Le Joueur* (tr. Sylvie Luneau), Paris: Gallimard, 1958; also in Aa24, pp.17-33; also in Aa67, pp.120-9.

Ab108 'Joyce et le roman moderne', *Les Lettres Françaises*, 863 (16.2.61), 1, 3; also in *L'Arc*, 36 (1968), 4-5.

Ab109 'Kujawski à Darmstadt', *Les Lettres Nouvelles*, 16 (July 61), 140-3.

Ab110 'Lautréamont court métrage', in Aa70, pp.245-57; also as film.

Ab111 'Lectures de l'enfance', *L'Arc*, 29 (1966), 43-5; also in Aa69, pp.259-62.

Ab112 'Lettre à Jean-Luc Parant', *Obliques*, 1 (1972), 105; also in Aa32, pp.117-18; also in Ab44.

Ab113 'Les Libertés du romanesque; à l'occasion de la publication de *La Révocation de l'édit de Nantes* de Pierre Klossowski', *Arts*, 717 (8.4.59), 3.

Ab114 'Litanie d'eau', in Aa30, pp.107-87; also in Aa52; also as Aa37.

Ab115 'La Littérature aujourd'hui, IV', *Tel Quel*, 11 (Aut. 62), 58-65; also under title 'Réponses à *Tel Quel*', in Aa22, pp.173-84 and Aa68, pp.293-301.

Ab116 'La Littérature, l'oreille et l'oeil', in Aa69, pp.391-403.

Ab117 'Littérature de témoignage ou littérature d'imagination?' (debate), *Les Nouvelles Littéraires*, 1799 (22.2.62), 6-7.

Ab118 'Le Livre comme objet', *Critique*, XVIII, 186 (Nov. 62), 929-46; also in Aa22, pp.130-57; also in Aa68, pp.104-23.

Ab119 'Le Livre et la musique' in Pierre Barbéris, Roland Barthes, MB *et al, Ecrire pour quoi? pour qui? Dialogues de France-Culture, no. 2*, Grenoble: Presses Universitaires de Grenoble, 1972.

'Livres imaginaires', see Ab21.

'Louqsor', see Ab63.

'Les Machines imaginaires', see Ab21.

Ab120* 'Les Machines sont des liens parmi nous', in *Les Peintres témoins de leur temps*, VIII: *L'Age mécanique*, Paris: Musée Galliéra, 1959, pp.66-71.

'Magritte et les mots', see Ab137.

Ab121 'Mallarmé selon Boulez', *L'Express*, 523 (22.6.61), 46; also in Aa24, pp.95-109; also in Aa68, pp.243-51.

Ab122 'Mallia', in Aa25, pp.92-4; also under title 'L'Hospitalité de Mallia', *Les Nouvelles Littéraires*, 1579 (5.12.57), 9.

Ab123 'Mantoue', in Aa25, pp.95-100; also under title 'La Splendeur de Mantoue', *France-Observateur*, 395 (5.12.57), 24.

'La Marque et le don', see Ab137.

Ab124 'Maryvonne (Daniel) ou le wagon maudit', *France-Observateur*, 389 (24.10.57), 15-16.

Ab125 'Maupassant: les jeunes écrivains ne le méprisent plus', *Arts*, 899 (9.1.63), 3.

Ab126   '*Max Ernst*', *Critique*, XV, 151 (Dec. 59), 1049-59.

Ab127   'Max Ernst: *Ecritures*', *Les Cahiers du Chemin*, 11 (15.1. 71), 164-74; also under title 'Ce que dit *La Femme 100 têtes*', in Aa70, pp. 323-9.

Ab128   'Méditation explosée', *Les Cahiers du Chemin*, 17 (15.1. 73), 20-45; also in Aa32, pp.10-153.

Ab129   'MB a-t-il tiré Claude Monet vers l'informel?', *Les Lettres Françaises*, 965 (14.2.63), 1.

'MB relit Balzac', see Ab168.

'MB relit Cervantes', see Ab145.

Ab130   'Missive mi-vive', in Aa32, pp.15-148.

Ab131   'Mode et moderne', *Change*, 4 (1969); also in Aa70, pp.399-414.

Ab132   'Les *Moments* de Marcel Proust', *Monde Nouveau*, 95 (Dec. 55), 125-35; also in Aa24, pp.111-28; also in Aa67, pp.163-72; also in *Les Critiques de notre temps et Proust*, ed. Jacques Bersani, Paris: Garnier Frères, 1971, pp.116-28.

Ab133   'Mon Journal à l'heure des prix', *Arts*, 647 (4.2.57), 5.

'Les Montagnes Rocheuses', see Ab4.

'Montaigne, cet enfant prodige', see Ab159.

'Montaigne dans le troisième livre des *Essais*', see Ab159.

Ab134   'Monument de rien pour Apollinaire', *La Nouvelle Revue Française*, 147 (Mar. 65), 503-14; 148 (Apr. 65), 604-708; also in Aa69, pp.269-305. CR: see Bb192.

Ab135   'Les Mosquées de New York ou l'art de Mark Rothko', *Critique*, XVIII, 173 (Oct. 61), 843-60; also in Aa69, pp.351-69.

Ab136   'Les Mots à la presse', in Aa52, p.121.

Ab137   'Les Mots dans la peinture', in Aa70, pp.31-95; also as Aa51. Extracts under title 'L'Inscription dans le portrait', *Manteia*, 6 (1969); 'Magritte et les mots', *Les Lettres Françaises*, 1257 (13.11.68), 7-8; 'La Marque et le don', *Les Cahiers du Chemin*, 6 (15.4.69), 74-86.

Ab138   'Mouvement brownien', in Aa2; also extract under title 'Traces' in *Les Lettres Françaises*, 759 (5.2.59), 1, 9; and as 'Poèmes anciens', *Les Lettres Nouvelles*, 68 (Feb. 59), 190-202 [dated 1948].

Ab139   'Mur-murmure', in Aa52, pp.130-2.

Ab140   'La Musique, art réaliste: les paroles et la musique', *Esprit*, XXVIII, 280 (Jan. 60), 138-56; also in Aa68, pp.27-41.

Ab141   'La Mystique du surhomme', *La Vie Intellectuelle*, 11 (Nov. 48), 141-2.

Ab142   'La Neige entre Bloomfield et Bernalillo', *Les Cahiers du Chemin*, 9 (15.10.70), 106-62; also in different form in Aa56, pp.129-256.

Ab143   'Neuf autres vues du mont Sandia', in Aa56, pp.39-370.

Ab144*   'Notes autour de Mondrian', introduction to *Tout l'œuvre peint de Mondrian*, Paris: Flammarion, 1976.

Ab145   'Les Nouvelles exemplaires', in Aa68, pp.139-45. Extract under title 'MB relit Cervantes', *Les Nouvelles Littéraires*, 1779 (5.10.61), 1, 6.

Ab146   'Nuage', in Aa52, p.125.

Ab147   'Octal', in Aa33, pp.54-104.

Ab148   'L'Oeil de MB sur Canaletto', *Réalités*, 258 (July 67), 36-43.

Ab149   'L'Oeil des Sargasses', in Aa33, pp.8-32; also as Aa53.

Ab150   'Une Œuvre articulée', *Arts et Loisirs*, 57 (26.10.66), 29.

Ab151   'L'Œuvre-mot', *Silex* (Grenoble), 2 (Jan. 77), 125.

         'Les Œuvres d'art imaginaires', in Ab21.

Ab152   'Les Œuvres d'art imaginaires chez Proust', in Aa24, pp.129-97; also as Aa54; also in Aa68, pp.252-92.

Ab153   'Une Œuvre solitaire', *Monde Nouveau*, 98 (Mar. 56), 91-6.

Ab154   'Ombres d'une île', introduction to *Ombres d'une île*, Paris: Bélier-Prisma, 1966; also in Aa31, pp.226-57, 230-47, 232-44.

Ab155   'L'Opéra, c'est-à-dire le théâtre', *L'Arc*, 27 (1965), 81-6; also in Aa69, pp.383-90.

Ab156   'L'Opinion des écrivains (sur le procès de Jérôme Lindon)', *Les Lettres Françaises*, 907 (28.12.61), 4.

Ab157   'Opusculum baudelairianium', in Aa70, pp.237-44.

Ab158   'Organiser des images des sons avec des mots', in *Les Critiques de notre temps et le nouveau roman*, ed. Réal Ouellet, Paris: Garnier Frères, 1972, pp.19-20.

Ab159   'L'Origine des *Essais*, la suite des *Essais*, le monde des *Essais*', preface to Montaigne, *Essais*, Paris: Union Générale d'Editions, 1964, 3 vols; also as Aa23; also extracts under title 'Montaigne, cet enfant prodige', *L'Express*, 700 (16. 11.64), 74-5, 'Montaigne dans le troisième livre des *Essais*', *Les Lettres Nouvelles*, 53 (Jan. 65), 16-44, 'Le Second Livre des *Essais*', *Critique*, XX, 210 (Nov. 64), 920-42. CR: see Bb481.

Ab160   'Orly en poésie', *L'Express*, 596 (15.11.62), 34; also as part of Aa71.

Ab161   'Où allez-vous pour rire?', *Les Nouvelles Littéraires*, 1795 (25.1.62), 12.

Ab162   'Où j'apprends', *Le Français dans le Monde*, 77 (Dec. 70), 8-9.

Ab163   'Palerme', *L'Arc*, 6 (1959), 77-80.

Ab164   'Parade des sournois', in Aa70, pp.341-9; also in *Les Lettres Françaises*, 1126 (7.4.65); also as introduction to Saul Steinberg, *Le Masque*, Paris: Maeght, 1966.

Ab165   'Les Paradis artificiels', in Aa24, pp.7-15; also in Aa67, pp.115-9; extract in *Arts*, 757 (13.1.60), 4.

Ab166   'Les Paravents', *Obliques*, 2 (1972), 54-9.

Ab167 * 'Les Parenthèses de l'été', *Encres Vives*, 67 (Aut.-Wint. 69); also in Aa33, pp.112-33; also in Alain Bosquet & Pierre Seghers, *Les Poèmes de l'année*, Paris: Seghers, 1970.

Ab168   'Les Parents pauvres', in Aa68, pp.193-8; extract under title 'MB relit Balzac', *Les Nouvelles Littéraires*, 1784 (9.11.61), 1, 5.

Ab169   'Les Parisiens en province', postface to Honoré de Balzac, *L'Illustre Gaudissart. La Muse du département*, Paris: Mazenod, 1967; also in Aa69, pp.169-83.

'Le Parler populaire et les langues anciennes', see Ab85.

'Le Paysage de la vallée', see Ab63.

Ab170 'Paysage de répons', *Les Lettres Françaises*, 1175 (23.3.67), 3-4; also in *Phantomas*, 63-7 (Dec. 66); also in Aa31; also in Aa59; also in Aa51; also in different form as part of Aa84; also as part of Ab171.

Ab171 '"Paysage de répons" illustré par "Dialogue des règnes"', in Aa84, pp.85-129; also as Aa59. Contains Ab64, 170 (extract).

Ab172 'Peindre une vague', in Aa52, pp.17-18.

Ab173* 'La Peinture se repeuple', *Figures* (New York), 1 (Sept. 61), 4-21.

Ab174* 'La Peinture surréaliste', *Cahier Bicolore* (Paris), 4 (Mar. 63), 23-8.

Ab175 'Pérégrination', *Tel Quel*, 7 (Aut. 61), 67-75; also in Aa84, pp.25-39.

Ab176 'Perle', *Métamorphoses*, 15-16 (May 71); also in Aa33, pp.12-13, 36-7, 50-1, 74-5, 108-9, 126-7.

Ab177 'Petite Croisière préliminaire à une reconnaissance de l'archipel Joyce', *La Vie Intellectuelle*, XVI, 5 (May 48), 104-35; also in Aa24, pp.239-81; also in Aa67, pp.195-218.

Ab178 'Petites Liturgies intimes pour hâter l'avènement des grands transparents de Jacques Hérold', *Les Cahiers du Chemin*, 15 (15.4.72), 173-80; also under title 'Petites Liturgies pour hâter l'avènement du grand transparent de Jacques Hérold', in Aa32, pp.72-92; also as Aa60.

Ab179 'Petit vocabulaire d'automne', in Eugène Guillevic, Alain Bosquet, MB, Marcel Béalu, *Saisons*, illus. Robert Blanchet, Boulogne-sur-Seine: Blanchet, 1972.

Ab180 '"Philosophie de l'ameublement"', *L'Express*, 659 (30.1. 64); also in Aa22, pp.59-72; also in Aa68, pp.51-60.

Ab181 *'Philosophie de Virginia Woolf par Maxime Chastaing', Monde Nouveau Paru*, 62 (1952), 99 [signed M.B.].

Ab182 'Pierre Klossowski: Une vocation suspendue', *Le Monde*, 6354 (19.6.65), 14.

Ab183 'La Place Saint-Marc', *Livres de France*, 6 (June-July 63); also in Aa14.

Ab184 '*Le Planétarium*, le jeu compliqué des paroles et des silences', *Arts*, 725 (3.6.59), 2.

   'La Pluie à Angkor', see Ab22.

Ab185 'Poème écrit en Egypte', *Les Cahiers du Sud*, XLVI, 351 (July 59), 203-12; also in Aa84, pp.73-81 [dated 1951].

   'Poèmes anciens', see Ab138.

Ab186 'Poème optique (sur les logogrammes de Christian Dotremont)', *Strates*, 7 (1966); also in Aa31, pp.1-262.

Ab187 '*Les Poésies* de Georges Schehadé', *Monde Nouveau Paru*, 62 (1952), 92-3.

Ab188* 'Le Point suprême et l'âge d'or à travers quelques œuvres de Jules Verne', *Arts et Lettres*, 15 (1949), 3-31; also in Aa24, pp.35-94; also in Aa67, pp.130-62.

Ab189* 'La Politique des charmeuses', *Métamorphoses*, 9 (1969); also in *Topique*, 4-5 (Oct. 70), 99-101; also as Aa33, pp.114-21; also as Aa62.

Ab190 'Une Possibilité', *Monde Nouveau*, 97 (Feb 56), 124-30; also in Aa67, pp.110-14.

Ab191 'Pour Denise', *L'Arc*, 43 (1970), 21-4; also under title 'Aveux', in Aa70, pp.415-19.

Ab192* 'Pour Gregory Masurovsky', *Pour l'Art*, 75 (Nov.-Dec. 60), 12-15.

Ab193* 'Pourquoi et comment lisez-vous?', *Cercle Ouvert* (9.10.65),5.

Ab194 '*Le Préau* par Georges Borgeaud', *Monde Nouveau Paru*, 59 (1952), 58-60 [signed M.B.].

Ab195 'Préface' to Guillaume Apollinaire, *Calligrammes: Poèmes de la paix et de la guerre, 1913-1916*, Paris: Gallimard, 1966.

Ab196 'Préface' to William Styron, *La Proie des flammes*, tr. M. E. Coindreau, Paris: Gallimard, 1962.

Ab197 'Première vue de Philadelphie', *Bryn Mawr Alumnae Bulletin*, 3 (Spr. 60), 8-9; also in *Les Lettres Nouvelles*, 9 (Dec. 60), 153-5.

   'Printemps en Haute-Egypte', see Ab63.

Ab198 'Propos sur l'écriture et la typographie', *Communication et Langages*, 13 (Mar. 72), 5-29.

Ab199   'Propos sur le livre aujourd'hui', *Les Cahiers du Chemin*, 12 (15.4.71), 44-60; also in Aa70, pp.431-43.

Ab200   'La Prosodie de Villon', *Critique*, XXIX, 310 (Mar. 73), 195-214; also in Aa70, pp.97-119. CR: see Bb424.

Ab201   'Quatre Lettres écrites du Nouveau-Mexique à Camille Bryen', *Les Cahiers du Chemin*, 13 (15.10.71), 47-54; also in Aa32, pp.27-136; also as Aa36.

Ab202   'Qu'est-ce que l'avant-garde en 1958?', *Les Lettres Françaises*, 713 (13.3.58), 1.

Ab203   'Qu'est-ce que la pornographie?', *Les Lettres Françaises*, 894 (28.9.61), 1, 6.

Ab204   'Rabelais', in Aa68, pp.135-8.

'Rabelais et les hiéroglyphes', see Ab85.

Ab205   'Racine et les dieux', *Les Lettres Nouvelles*, 15 (10.6.59), 18-27; 16 (17.6.59), 41-51; also in Aa67, pp.28-60. Extracts in *Les Lettres Françaises*, 796 (29.10.59), 1, 7.

Ab206   'Rat-lièvre-hareng', *Les Cahiers des Saisons*, 18 (Aut. 59), 288-9, 290-1, 291-3 [dated 1955].

Ab207   '*Raymond Roussel* par Jean Ferry', *La Nouvelle Nouvelle Revue Française*, 16 (Apr. 54), 711-3.

Ab208   'Recherches sur la technique du roman', *Les Lettres Françaises*, 1008 (19.12.53), 1, 5; also in Aa22, pp.109-29; also in Aa68, pp.88-99.

Ab209   'Reconnaissance', *Le Figaro Littéraire*, 918 (21.11.63), 7.

Ab210*   'Regard double sur Berlin', *L'Express*, 707 (4.1.65), 51-3; also in Aa31, pp.2-37, 6-9, 16-30; also as introduction to *Die ganze Stadt Berlin*, Hamburg: Nonnen, 1963.

Ab211   'Les Relations de parenté dans *L'Ours* de William Faulkner', *Les Lettres Nouvelles*, 38 (May 56), 734-45; also in Aa24, pp.339-60; also in Aa67, pp.250-61.

Ab212   'Remarques', in Cesare Peverelli, *Répertoire I (1957-60)*, Montpellier: Fata Morgana, 1972; also in Aa32, pp.47-116.

Ab213   'Rencontre', in Aa30, pp.31-53; also as Aa66. Extract in *Les Lettres Nouvelles*, 29 (Oct. 62), 31-5.

Ab214   'Rencontre avec Antonioni', *Les Lettres Françaises*, 880 (15.6.61), 1, 7; also as preface to Antonioni, *La Nuit*, tr. Michèle Causse, Paris: Buchet-Castel, 1961.*

Ab215   'La Répétition', *Monde Nouveau Paru* (1950); also in Aa67, pp.94-109.

'Réponses à *Tel Quel*', see Ab115.

Ab216   'Reproduction interdite', *Critique*, XXXI, 334 (Mar. 75), 269-83.

Ab217* 'Ressac', in Veira da Silva, *Les Irrésolutions résolues*, Paris: Editions Jeanne Bucher, 1969; also in *La Nouvelle Revue Française*, 212 (Aug. 70), 19-20; also in Alain Bosquet & Pierre Seghers, *Les Poèmes de l'année, 1971*, Paris: Seghers, 1971.

Ab218   'Le Rêve de l'ammonite', in Aa40, pp.39-72; also as Aa72.

Ab219   'Le Rêve de Bernard Saby', *Les Cahiers du Chemin*, 27 (15.4.76), 59-81.

Ab220   'Le Rêve de boules et d'yeux', in Aa76, pp.183-218.

Ab221   'Le Rêve du déménagement', in Aa40, pp.73-98.

Ab222   'Le Rêve de l'huître', *Les Cahiers du Chemin*, 22 (15.10. 74), 55-74; also in Aa40, pp.9-38.

Ab223   'Le Rêve de la montagne noire', in Aa76, pp.100-37.

Ab224   'Le Rêve de l'ombre', in Aa76, pp.138-82; also as Aa73.

Ab225   'Le Rêve de Paul Delvaux', *Les Cahiers du Chemin*, 23 (15.1.75), 52-73; also in Aa13; also under title 'Le Rêve de Vénus', in Aa76, pp.9-56.

Ab226   'Le Rêve de Prague', in Aa40, pp.99-121.

Ab227   'Le Rêve des ombres', in Aa76, pp.57-99.

Ab228   'Le Rêve des souffles', *Les Cahiers du Chemin*, 29 (15.1. 77), 62-77.

Ab229   'Le Rêve du tatouage', in Aa40, pp.122-37.

'Le Rêve de Vénus', see Ab225.

Ab230   'Rien à déclarer', in Aa52, p.124.

Ab231   'Le Rôle de l'écrivain', *L'Express*, 423 (23.7.59), 25-7.

Ab232   'Le Roman comme recherche', *Les Cahiers du Sud*, XLIII,

334 (Apr. 56), 349-54; also in Aa22, pp.7-14; also in Aa67, pp.7-11; also in Maurice Nadeau, *Le Roman français depuis la guerre*, Paris: Gallimard, 1963, pp.288-93

Ab233   'Le Roman, l'épreuve du temps', *Arts*, 732 (23.7.59), 3.

Ab234   'Le Roman est un laboratoire du récit', *Les Lettres Françaises*, 661 (7.3.57), 1, 3.

Ab235   'Le Roman et la poésie', *Les Lettres Nouvelles*, 11 (Feb. 61), 47-65; also in *Annales du Centre Universitaire Méditerranéen*', XV (1961-2), 219-29; also in Aa22; also in Aa68, pp.7-26.

Ab236   'Sablier', in Aa52, p.133.

Ab237   '*Sainte Barbegrise* de Noël Delvaux', *Monde Nouveau Paru*, 63 (1952), 81.

Ab238   'Salonique', *La Nouvelle Nouvelle Revue Française*, 48 (Dec. 56), 979-88; also in Aa25, pp.41-57.

Ab239   'Sans feu ni lieu', *Australian Journal of French Studies*, XI, 3 (Sept.-Dec. 74), 325-40.

'Le Second livre des *Essais*', see Ab159.

Ab240   'Les Sept Femmes de Gilbert le Mauvais', *L'Arc*, 47 (1971), 33-45; also in Aa70, pp.293-322; also as Aa78.

Ab241   'Sites', in Aa69, pp.25-31; also as preface to Jean Richer, *Géographie sacrée du monde grec. Croyances astrales des anciens Grecs*, Paris: Hachette, 1966.

'6/7 ou les dés de Rabelais', see Ab85.

Ab242   'Sous le regard d'Hercule', *La Nouvelle Revue Française*, 153 (Sept. 65), 494-506; also in Aa69, pp.371-81.

Ab243   'Souvenirs d'enfance', *L'VII*, 5 (21.4.61), 9-30.

'Spectacles imaginaires', see Ab21.

Ab244   'Spirale', *Quadrum*, 19 (1965), 107-14; also in Aa31; also as Aa80.

Ab245   'La Spirale des sept péchés', *Critique*, XVI, 276 (May 70), 387-412; also in Aa70, pp.209-35; extract under title 'La Forme de la tentation', *Esprit Créateur*, X, 1 (Spr. 70), 3-12.

'La Splendeur de Mantoue', see Ab123.

'Suggestions', see Ab21.

Ab246   'La Suite dans les images', *Les Lettres Françaises*, 898 (26.10.61), 9; also in Aa69, pp.263-8.

'La Suite des *Essais*', see Ab159.

Ab247   'Sur l'archéologie', in Aa69, pp.21-4.

Ab248   'Sur la déclaration dite "des 121"', in Aa22, pp.158-61; also in Aa68, pp.124-6.

Ab249   'Sur *Les Liaisons dangereuses*', *Les Lettres Françaises*, 1000 (24.10.63), 11; also in Aa68, pp.146-51.

Ab250   'Sur mon visage', *Les Cahiers du Chemin*, 18 (15.4.73), 135-8; also in Aa70, pp.421-3.

'Sur la page', see Ab89.

Ab251   'Sur *La Princesse de Clèves*', *Les Lettres Françaises*, 769 (16.4.59), 1, 11; also in Aa67, pp.74-8.

Ab252   'Sur les procédés de Raymond Roussel', in Aa24, pp.199-221; also in Aa67, pp.173-85; extract in *Rixes*, 1 (May-June 50), 10-12.*

Ab253   'Sur *Le Progrès de l'âme* de John Donne', *Les Cahiers du Sud*, XLI, 321 (Jan. 54), 276-85; also in Aa67, pp.20-7.

Ab254   'Des Symptômes d'époque', *Arts*, 870 (18.4.62), 3.

Ab255   'Un Tableau vu en détail', *Monde Nouveau*, 101 (June 56), 83-92; also in Aa69, pp.33-41.

Ab256   'La Tentative poétique d'Ezra Pound', *Critique*, XII, 106 (Mar. 56), 734-45; also in Aa24, pp.311-37; also in Aa67, pp.234-49.

Ab257   'Le Théâtre de Victor Hugo, I, II, III', *La Nouvelle Revue Française*, 143 (Nov. 64), 862-78; 144 (Dec. 64), 1073-82; 145 (Jan. 65), 105-13; also under title 'La Voix qui sort de l'ombre et le poison qui transpire à travers les murs', in Aa69, pp.185-213.

Ab258   'Tolstoï devant les écrivains d'aujourd'hui', *Les Lettres Françaises*, 843 (29.9.60), 1, 4.

Ab259   'Tourmente', in Aa33, pp.58-69; also as Aa83.

'Traces', see Ab138.

Ab260   'Transfiguration', in Aa70, pp.331-9.

Ab261   '35 Vues du mont Sandia le soir l'hiver', in Aa56, pp.11-24, 59-80, 89-114, 119-54, 213-390.

Ab262   'Trente-six et dix vues du Fuji', in Aa69, pp.159-68; extracts under title 'Hokusaï', *Les Lettres Françaises*, 860 (26.1.61), 10; 'Hokusaï II', *Réalités*, 187 (Aug. 61), 20-9.

'Trille Transparent Tremble', see Ab264.

Ab263   'Trois hommages (Charlie Parker, Murnau, Mitchourine)', *Les Cahiers du Sud*, LIII, 387-8 (Apr.-June 66), 227-32; also in Alain Bosquet & Pierre Seghers, *Les Poèmes de l'année*, Paris: Seghers, 1967.

Ab264*   'Trouble Tremble Transparent Trille', *L'Arbre*, 8-9 (July-Oct. 68), 7-12; also under title 'Trille Transparent Tremble', in Aa33, pp. 78-122.

Ab265   'L'Usage des pronoms personnels dans le roman', *Les Temps Modernes*, 178 (Feb. 61), 936-48; also in Aa22, pp.73-88; also in Aa68, pp.61-72.

Ab266   'Variations sur un rêve primitif', *Le Figaro Littéraire*, 1504 (15.3.75), 11.

Ab267   'Veilleuse-brûlot', in Aa52, p.126.

'La Vendeuse des Galeries Lafayette', see Ab21.

Ab268   'Vers un nouveau romantisme', *Arts*, 700 (10.12.58), 3.

Ab269*   'Le Vestibule de Saint-Marc (l'arche de Noé)', *Sandorama* (Aut. 63); also in Aa14.

Ab270   'Le Vestibule de Saint-Marc (la coupole de la création)', *La Nouvelle Revue Française*, 118 (Oct. 62), 593-604; also in Aa14.

Ab271   'Le Vestibule de Saint-Marc (l'histoire de Joseph)', *Les Cahiers du Sud*, L, 372 (July-Aug. 63), 195-207; also in Aa14.

Ab272   'Victor Hugo critique', *Critique*, XXI, 221 (Oct. 65), 803-26; also under title 'Germe d'encre', in Aa69, pp.215-39.

Ab273   'Victor Hugo romancier', *Tel Quel*, 16 (Wint. 64), 60-77; also in Aa68, pp.215-42.

'Les Villes imaginaires', see Ab21.

Ab274   'La Voix de l'écrit, cantate pour saluer les logogrammes de

Christian Dotremont', *La Nouvelle Revue Française*, 212 (Aug. 70), 23-5.

'La Voix qui sort de l'ombre et le poison qui transpire à travers les murs', see Ab257.

Ab275 'Votre Faust fantaisie variable genre opéra', *La Nouvelle Revue Française*, 109 (Jan. 62), 65-86; 110 (Feb. 62), 261-89; 111 (Mar. 62), 461-82; 112 (Apr. 62), 641-57. Other versions in Ab281; *Les Cahiers du Centre d'Etudes et de Recherches Marxistes*, 62 (1968); *Les Cahiers de la Compagnie Madeleine Renaud—Jean-Louis Barrault*, 42-3 (Feb.-Dec. 63),   203-15; *Médiations*, 6 (Summ. 63), 5-20*; *Profils*, 2 (Nov. 62),   23-25*; also as Aa89.

Ab276 'Le Voyage et l'écriture', in Aa70, pp.9-29.

Ab277 'Vues célestes', *Alif* (Tunis), 7 (Wint. 76), 5-6;   also in Aa52, p.127.

Ab278 'Western Duo', *The Malahat Review*, 36 (Oct. 75), 65-74; also in Aa33, pp.40-70; also as Aa90.

Ab279 'William Faulkner, son pays a mis longtemps à le comprendre', *Le Figaro Littéraire*, 847 (14.7.62), 8.

'Zola et l'expérimentation romanesque', see Ab66.

Ab280* 'Zoo', *Avant-Quart*, 19 (1970).

Ab281 *L'VII*, 10 (June 62), partly devoted to MB.   Contains Ab17, 138 and one version of Ab275.

Almansi, G., see Ac3.

Ac1   Arban, Dominique, 'Cinq minutes avec MB', *Le Figaro Littéraire*, 555 (17.11.56), 12.

Ac2   Bajomée, Danielle, 'Huit questions à MB', *Marche Romane*, XXI (1971), 37-9.

Ac3   Bann, Stephen, and G. Almansi, 'Interview with MB', *20th Century Studies*, 6 (Dec. 71), 41-52.

Ac4   Borderie, Roger, 'Entretien avec MB', *Les Lettres Françaises*, 1315 (31.12.69), 7-8.

Ac5   ——, 'La Revanche de Zola: Entretien', *Le Nouvel Observateur*, 122 (15.3.67), 32-3.

Ac6   ——, '*Travaux d'approche* par MB. Entretien', *Obliques*, 2 (1972), 87-90; also in Aa84, pp.7-19.

Ac7   ——, and Henri Ronse, 'Dramaturgie pour un théâtre mobile: un entretien avec MB', *Les Lettres Françaises*, 1225 (13.3. 68), 14-15.

Ac8   Boulanger, Nicole, 'Les Sept Chambres de Marcel', *Le Nouvel Observateur*, 347 (5.7.71), 10-11.

Ac9   Bourgeade, P., 'Entretien avec MB', in *Violoncelle qui résiste*, Paris: Losfeld, 1971, pp.127-36.

Ac10   Bourin, André, 'Les Enfants du demi-siècle: MB', *Les Nouvelles Littéraires*, 1579 (5.12.57), 9.

Ac11*   ——, 'Instantané', *Les Nouvelles Littéraires*, 1553 (17.1.57), 17.

Ac12   Cadieu, Martine, 'Entretien avec MB', *Les Lettres Françaises*, 1168 (2.2.67), 16-17.

Ac13   ——, 'Le Nouvel opéra. Entretien avec MB et Henri Pousseur', *Les Nouvelles Littéraires*, 2159 (6.2.59), 11.

Ac14   Caruso, Paulo, 'Intervista a MB', *Aut Aut*, 68 (Mar. 62), 165-7.

Ac15*   Chadeau, Danielle, 'MB enfante un nouveau monstre: *Mobile*', *Démocratie*, 68 (8.3.62), 19.

Ac16   Chapsal, Madeleine, 'Entretien: MB', *L'Express*, 561 (15.3. 62), 32-4.

Ac17   —, 'MB', in *Ecrivains en personne*, Paris: René Julliard, 1960, pp.55-70.

Ac18   —, 'MB à Grenoble', *La Quinzaine Littéraire*, 44 (1.2.68), 14-15.

Ac19   Charbonnier, Georges, *Entretiens avec MB*, Paris: Gallimard, 1967 (Broadcast on France-Culture, Jan.-Feb. 1967). CR: see Bb8, 187, 293, 344, 446, 729.

Ac20   Clec'h, Guy le, 'Entretien avec MB. La Littérature, fille du roman. Un rempart contre le monde', *Les Nouvelles Littéraires*, 2283 (25.6.71), 9.

Ac21   Craipeau, Maria, 'Entretien avec MB', *France-Observateur*, 506 (14.1.60), 19.

Ac22   Daix, Pierre, 'Entretiens sur l'art actuel', *Les Lettres Françaises*, 1037 (9.7.64), 1, 6.

Ac23   Epenoux, Christian d', 'Interview de MB', *Arts-Spectacles*, 647 (14.12.57), 4.

Ac24   Fabre-Luce, Anne, and Georges Raillard, 'Du mouvement en littérature. Entretien avec MB', *Cahiers du XXᵉ Siècle*, 1 (1973), 7-23.

Ac25   Forrester, Vivianne, 'Philtres et filtres de MB', *Le Nouvel Observateur*, 544 (14.4.75), 72-3.

Ac26   Gaugeard, Jean, 'Entretien avec MB sur son œuvre', *Les Lettres Françaises*, 1022 (26.3.64), 4.

Ac27*   Guth, Paul, 'Un Révolutionnaire du roman', *Le Figaro Littéraire*, 607 (7.12.57), 1, 9.

Ac28   Helbo, André, 'Dialogue avec MB', in Ba14, pp.9-15.

Ac29*   Jamous, Albert, 'Rencontre avec MB', *L'Orient* (7.5.62).

Ac30   Jeancard, Pierre, 'Vers un enseignement universel: Entretien avec MB', *Liberté*, X, 2 (Mar.-Apr. 68), 33-7.

Ac31   Jolas, Paul, 'Questionnaire de M. Jolas adressé à MB', *Rencontres Artistiques et Littéraires*, 5 (June 72), 12.

Ac32   Juin, Hubert, 'Une Heure de cours d'histoire . . . interview de MB', *Les Lettres Françaises*, 807 (14.1.60), 5.

Ac33   Kolbert, Jack, 'An Interview with MB', *The American Society of the Legion of Honor Magazine*, XLV, 2 (1974), 90-3.

Ac34 Masurovsky, Gregory, 'Un Entretien avec MB', *Opus International*, 26 (June 71).

Ac35 Melançon, Robert, 'Entretien avec MB' [6.8.74, Middlebury, Vermont], *Etudes Françaises* (Montreal), XI (Feb. 75), 67-92.

Ac36 Peillard, Léonce, 'Léonce Peillard s'entretient avec MB', *Livres de France*, 6 (June-July 63), 6-8.

Ac37 Piatier, Jacqueline, 'MB s'explique', *Le Monde*, 6902 (22.3. 67), V.

Ac38 Pivot, Bernard, 'MB a réponse à tous', *Le Figaro Littéraire*, 1307 (4.6.71), II.

Ac39 Q[uéant], G[illes], 'Un Art nouveau? MB nous éclaire sur les recherches d'aujourd'hui', *Plaisir de France*, 368 (June 69), 1-5.

Ac40 Raillard, Georges, 'Entretien de Georges Raillard avec MB', in Ba28, pp.263-9.

Ac41 Rambures, Jean-Louis de, 'Comment travaillent les écrivains. MB une entreprise de dédoublement de la personnalité', *Le Monde*, 8213 (11.6.71), 24.

Ac42 Ronse, Henri, 'Le Livre futur: Entretien avec MB', *Synthèses*, 248 (Jan. 67), 101-7.

Ac43 —, 'MB: "Je ne suis pas iconoclaste"', *Les Lettres Françaises*, 1178 (13.4.67), 5.

Ac44 Saint-Aubyn, F. C., 'A propos de *Mobile*. Deuxième entretien avec MB', *French Review*, XXXVIII, 4 (Feb. 64), 427-40.

Ac45 —, 'Entretien avec MB', *French Review*, XXXVI, 1 (1962), 12-22.

Ac46 Saint-Phalle, Thérèse de, 'MB commente *Mobile*', *Le Monde*, 5304 (14.2.62), 11.

Ac47 Sicard, Michel, 'MB au travail du texte', *Magazine Littéraire*, 110 (Mar. 76), 14-27.

Ac48 —, 'MB: matière de rêve et matière de l'art', *Magazine Littéraire*, 129 (Oct. 77), 54-6.

Ac49* Anon., 'MB en 40 questions', *La Galerie*, 106 (July 71), 64-5.

Ad TRANSLATIONS BY MB

Ad1   Gurwitsch, Aaron, *La Théorie du champ de la conscience*, Brussels: Desclée de Brouwer, 1957.

Ad2   Lukács, Georg, *Brève Histoire de la littérature allemande* (tr. with Lucien Goldmann), Paris: Nagel, 1949.

Ad3   Shakespeare, William, *Tout est bien qui finit bien*, Paris: Formes et Reflets, 1958.

Ae1   *A Change of Heart*, tr. Jean Stewart of Aa42, New York: Simon & Schuster, 1958, 249pp. Also in Ae8.
CR: see Bb348, 436, 497.

Ae2   *Degrees*, tr. Richard Howard of Aa12, New York: Simon & Schuster, 1961, 351pp; London: Methuen, 1962. 351pp.
CR: see Bb556, 733, 734.

Ae3   *Histoire Extraordinaire, Essay on a Dream of Baudelaire's*, tr. Richard Howard of Aa28, London: Jonathan Cape, 1969, 172pp.
CR: see Bb214.

Ae4   *Inventory*, tr. by various translators of parts of Aa67, Aa68, Aa69. Bb266 as preface, New York: Simon & Schuster, 1968, 318pp; London: Cape, 1970, 318pp.
Contains Ae9, 10, 11, 13, 16, 17, 20, 22, 23, 24, 25, 27, 28, 31, 32, 33, 36. CR: see Bb193, 502, 722.

Ae5   *Mobile, Study for a Representation of the United States*, tr. Richard Howard of Aa41, New York: Simon & Schuster, 1963, 319pp.

Ae6   *Niagara*, tr. Elinor S. Miller of Aa79, Chicago: Henry Regnery & Co., 1969, 267pp.
CR: see Bb621.

Ae7   *Passing Time*, tr. Jean Stewart of Aa20, London: Faber & Faber, 1960; New York: Simon & Schuster, 1960, 310pp; London: Calder, 1965, 310pp. Also in Ae8.
CR: see Bb288, 735.

Ae8   *Passing Time and A Change of Heart, Two Novels*, tr. Jean Stewart of Aa20 and Aa42. Repr. of Ae1 and Ae7, New York: Simon & Schuster, 1969, 561pp.
CR: see Bb736.

Ae9   'Balzac and Reality', tr. Remy Hall of Ab16 in Ae4, pp.100-13.

Ae10   'The Book as Object', tr. Patricia Dreyfus of Ab118 in Ae4, pp.39-56.

Ae11 'Chateaubriand and Early America', tr. Derek Coltman of Ab31 in Ae4, pp.59-99.

Ae12 'The Conversation. On Some Pictures of Alessandro Magnasco', tr. Edward Lucie-Smith of Ab38 in *French Writing Today*, ed. Simon Watson Taylor, Harmondsworth: Penguin, 1968, pp.230-7.

Ae13 'The Crisis in the Growth of Science Fiction', tr. Richard Howard of Ab45, *Partisan Review*, XXXIV (1967), 595-602; also in *S.F: The Other Side of Realism*, ed. Thomas D. Clareson, Bowling Green (Ohio): Univ. Press, 1971, pp. 157-65; also in Ae4, pp. 224-32.

Ae14 'Criticism and Invention', tr. Jean Garagnon and Graeme Watson of Ab46, *Meanjin Quarterly* (Melbourne), XXXVIII (1969), 461-71.

Ae15 'Crossing the Joycean Threshold', tr. Jerry A. Stewart of Ab177, *James Joyce Quarterly* (Oklahoma), 3 (Spr. 1970), 160-76.

Ae16 'Delphi', tr. Richard Howard of Ab52, *Evergreen Review*, 18 (May-June 61), 114-17, 119, 121-6; also in Ae4, pp.307-18.

Ae17 'The Golden Age in Jules Verne', tr. Patricia Dreyfus of Ab188 in Ae4, pp.114-45.

Ae18 'Growing Pains in Science Fiction', tr. Donald Schier of Ab45, *The Carleton Miscellany*, 3 (Summ. 63), 113-20.

Ae19 'Homage to Jules Verne', tr. of Ab90, *New Statesman*, 1844 (18.7.66), 84.

Ae20 'The Imaginary Works of Art in Proust', tr. Remy Hall of Ab152 in Ae4, pp.146-84.

Ae21 'Luxor', tr. Jean Stewart of extract from Ab63, *London Magazine*, X (1958), 14-22.

Ae22 'Mallarmé according to Boulez', tr. Michael Brozen of Ab121 in Ae4, pp.294-304.

Ae23 'Mondrian: The Square and its Inhabitant', tr. William Brown of Ab25 in Ae4, pp.235-52.

Ae24 'Monument of Nothing for Apollinaire', tr. Richard Howard of Ab134, *TriQuarterly* (Evanston, Illinois), IV (1965), 23-42; also in Ae4, pp.185-208.

Ae25 'Music, a Realistic Art', tr. Michael Brozen of Ab140 in Ae4, pp.281-93.

Ae26 'The Novel as Exploration', tr. A. M. Sheriden Smith of Ab232 in Maurice Nadeau, *The French Novel since the War*, New York: Grove Press, 1968, pp.168-93.

Ae27 'The Novel as Research', tr. Gerald Fabian of Ab232 in Ae4, pp.26-30; also in *Contemporary Writers on Modern Fiction*, ed. Malcolm Bradbury, Glasgow: Fontana, 1971, pp.48-53.

Ae28 'On Fairy Tales', tr. Remy Hall of Ab14 in Ae4, pp.211-23.

Ae29 *'Passage de Milan'*, tr. Guy Daniels of ch. VII-X of Aa57, in *The Award Avant-Garde Reader*, ed. Gil Orlovitz, New York: Award Books, 1965, pp.25-83.

Ae30 *'Passage de Milan'*, tr. Donald Schier of ch. XI-XII of Aa57, *The Carleton Miscellany*, 3 (Summ. 63), 121-32.

Ae31 'The Repopulation of the Painting', tr. Richard Howard of Ab173, in Ae4, pp.253-9.

Ae32 'Research on the Technique of the Novel', tr. Gerald Fabian of Ab208 in Ae4, pp.15-25.

Ae33 'Rothko: The Mosques of New York', tr. Richard Howard of Ab135 in Ae4, pp.260-77.

Ae34 'The Second Case: The Use of Personal Pronouns in the Novel', tr. of Ab265, *New Left Review*, 34 (Nov.-Dec. 65), 61-8.

Ae35 'Second Thoughts', extract from Ae1, *New Left Review*, 34 (Nov.-Dec. 65), 69-71.

Ae36 'The Space of the Novel', tr. Gerald Fabian of Ab69 in Ae4, pp.31-8.

Ae37 'Thoughts on the Novel: The Individual and the Group', tr. of Ab94, *Encounter*, XX, 6 (June 63), 17-23.

Ae38 'Zola's Blue Flame', tr. of Ab66, *Yale French Studies*, XLII (1969), 9-25.

B: SECONDARY MATERIAL

Ba BOOKS AND THESES

Ba1   Albérès, R.-M., *MB*, Paris: Editions Universitaires, Coll. Classiques du XXe Siècle, 1964, 124pp.
CR: see Bb121, 168, 309, 339, 391, 598, 730.

Ba2   *L'Arc*, 39 (1969), 104pp.
Contains Ab21; Bb69, 130, 316, 416, 463, 468, 495, 504, 537. CR: see Bb160, 352.

Ba3   Aubral, François, *MB. Une Introduction, un choix de textes, une bibliographie*, Paris: Seghers, Coll. Poètes d'Aujourd'hui, 209, 1973, 208pp.
Contains plates between pp.64-5, 105-6, 128-9, 176-7. Bb27 as introduction and Bb462 as preface. CR: see Bb517.

Ba4   Book-Senninger, Claude, and Jack Kolbert, *L'Art de MB*, New York: Oxford University Press, 1970, xx-183pp.
CR: see Bb54.

Ba5   Bousquet, Robert Edward, 'MB: Le Roman en tant qu'instrument de la transformation du réel', Ph.D. thesis, Georgetown Univ., 1970, 483pp. See Bb86.

Ba6   Bradshaw, J. A., 'Les Romans de MB', Ph.D. thesis, Univ. of Western Australia, 1973.

Ba7*   Calle-Gruber, Mireille, 'Thèmes et images du labyrinthe dans le Nouveau Roman: MB, Robbe-Grillet, Simon', Thèse de 3e Cycle, Univ. of Montpellier, 1974.

Charbonnier, Georges, see Ac19.

Ba8   Dällenbach, Lucien, *Le Livre et ses miroirs dans l'œuvre romanesque de MB*, Paris: Minard, Coll. Archives des Lettres Modernes, 135, 1972, 119pp.
Contains Bb145. CR: see Bb614.

Ba9   Dauer, Bernd, *Wirklichkeitsflucht und Entfremdung. Studien zur Erzählstruktur in den Romanen Alain Robbe-Grillets und MBs*, Heidelberg: Carl Winter Universitätsverlag, 1976.

Ba10   Grant, Marion A., *MB: L'Emploi du temps*, London: Edward Arnold, Coll. Studies in French Literature, XXVI, 1973, 62pp.

Ba11   Gregarias, Mary, 'MB and William Faulkner: some Structures and Techniques', Ph.D. thesis, Columbia Univ., 1968, 175pp. See Bb226.

Ba12   Hammond, Jeannine Lynette, 'MB and the Didactic Novel', Ph.D. thesis, Univ. of Indiana, 1973, 277pp. See Bb237.

Ba13   Hedges, Inez Kathleen, 'Temporal and Spatial Structures in Film and the Novel: a Comparison between Ozu Yasujiro's *Kohayagawe-ke no Aki* and MB's *L'Emploi du temps*, Ph.D thesis, Univ. of Wisconsin, Madison, 1976, 301pp. See Bb245.

Ba14   Helbo, André, *MB. Vers une littérature du signe*, Brussels: Complexe, Coll. Creusets, 181pp. Ac28 as preface.
        Contains Bb249.

Ba15   Howitt, J. B., 'England and the English in the Novels of MB', M.A. thesis, Univ. of Manchester, 1972.

        Kolbert, Jack, see Ba4.

Ba16   Kumm, Karl Ward Graham, 'MB: A Spatial Imagination', Ph.D. thesis, Univ. of Wisconsin, 1970, 427pp. See Bb336.

Ba17   Lalande, Bernard, *MB: La Modification. Analyse critique*, Paris: Hatier, 1972, 79pp.

Ba18   McWilliams, David Dean, 'The Influence of William Faulkner on MB', Ph.D. thesis, Univ. of Oregon, 1969, 162pp. See Bb377.

Ba19   Mason, Barbara J., 'Patterns of Narration in the Novels of MB', M.A. thesis, Univ. of Sussex, 1973, 120pp.

Ba20   ——, 'Structure and Symbol with Special Reference to Alchemy in the Works of MB', Ph.D. thesis, Univ. of Lancaster, 1977, 362pp.

Ba21   *MB, Centre Culturel Internationel de Cerisy-la-Salle*, Paris: U.G.E., Coll. 10/18, no. 902, 1973, 450pp.
        Contains Ab61; Bb28, 29, 80, 83, 149, 158, 320, 356, 375, 460, 501,

503, 508, 533, 547, 573, 607, 639, 662. CR: see Bb447.

Ba22   Nahnybida, Oksanna, 'From Mythology to Mythopoesis. Mythological Figures and Patterns in the Novels of MB', Ph.D. thesis, Tulane Univ., 1971, 170pp. See Bb430.

Ba23   O'Donnell, Thomas D., 'Joycean Themes and Techniques in the Works of MB', Ph.D. thesis, Univ. of Wisconsin, 1970, 266pp. See Bb437.

Ba24* Oseki, Inès, 'Les Recherches formelles dans l'œuvre de MB', Thèse de 3e Cycle, Univ. of Aix-Marseille, 1971, 481pp.

Ba25   Passias, Katharine, 'Structure and Movement in Three French New Novels, 1957-62. A Deep and a Surface Comparison', Ph. D. thesis, Univ. of Michigan, 1974, 417pp. See Bb454.

Ba26* Pottéra, Reto, 'MB. *Le Roman comme recherche*. Das Romanwerk in seiner Entwicklung', Ph.D. thesis, Univ. of Zurich, 1975, 193pp.

Ba27   Quéréel, Patrice, *'La Modification' de MB*, Paris: Hachette, Coll. Poche Critique, 1973, 94pp.

Ba28   Raillard, Georges, *MB*, Paris: Gallimard, Coll. La Bibliothèque Idéale, 1968, 317pp.
Contains Ac40; Bb513. CR: see Bb10, 11, 115, 319, 692, 698.

Ba29   Rice, Donald, 'Etude critique des romans de MB 1954-65', Ph.D. thesis, Univ. of Wisconsin, 1969, 354pp. See Bb526.

Ba30* Ross, Margaret Helen, 'L'Espace-temps dans le Nouveau Roman. Alain Robbe-Grillet, MB, Claude Simon', Thèse de 3e Cycle, Univ. of Orléans-Tours, 1970.

Ba31   Rossum-Guyon, Françoise van, *Critique du roman. Essai sur 'La Modification' de MB*, Ph.D. thesis, Univ. of Leiden; publ. Paris: Gallimard, Coll. Bibliothèque des Idées, 1970, 365pp.
CR: see Bb165, 189, 240, 254, 421, 482, 557, 622, 625-6, 646, 707.

Ba32   Roubichou, Gérard, *'La Modification'. Extraits avec une notice sur la vie et l'œuvre de MB, une étude de 'La Modification', des notes, des commentaires, des documents et des thèmes de réflexion*, Paris: Bordas, 1973, 190pp.

Ba33   Roudaut, Jean, *MB ou le livre futur*, Paris: Gallimard, Coll. Le Chemin, 1964, 242pp.
CR: see Bb45, 261, 721.

Ba34 Roudiez, Leon S., *MB*, New York and London: Columbia Univ. Press, Coll. Columbia Essays on Modern Writers, 1965, 48pp.
CR: see Bb289, 699.

Ba35 Smith, Esther Young, 'Crisis in the Novel: Max Frisch and MB', Ph.D. thesis, Indiana Univ., 1976, 219pp. See Bb600.

Ba36 Spencer, Michael C., *MB*, New York: Twayne's World Authors Series, 275, 1974, 187pp.
CR: see Bb225, 331, 365, 623, 737.

Ba37* *Textuerre* (Montpellier) [1977]. Devoted to MB.

Ba38* Thiele, Gisela, *Die Romane MBs : Untersuchungen zur Struktur von 'Passage de Milan', 'L'Emploi du temps', 'La Modification', 'Degrés'*, Heidelberg: Carl Winter, 1975, 208pp.

Van Rossum-Guyon, see Rossum-Guyon.

Ba39 Waelti-Walters, Jennifer (née Walters), *Alchimie et littérature, à propos de 'Portrait de l'artiste en jeune singe'*, Paris: Denoël, 1975, 178pp.

Ba40 ——, *MB: a Study of his View of the World and a Panorama of his Work 1954-74*, Victoria, B.C.: Sono Nis Press, 1977, 159pp.

Ba41 Walters, Jennifer, 'A Study of the Novels of MB', Ph.D. thesis, Univ. of London, 1968.

Ba42 Wolfzettel, Friedrich, *MB und der Kollektivroman. Von 'Passage de Milan' zu 'Degrés'*, Heidelberg: Carl Winter, 1969, 213pp.
CR: see Bb43, 183, 334.

Ba43* Anon., *MB et ses peintres* (catalogue), Brussels: Musée des Beaux-Arts, 1973, 43pp.
Catalogue of exhibition held at the Palais des Beaux-Arts, Le Havre, May 1973, then at the Musée des Beaux-Arts, Brussels, then at the Musée Masséna, Nice. This grouped works of several painters with whom MB has collaborated: Alechinsky, Bryen, Dotremont, Dufour, Francken, Kolar, Masson, Masurovsky, Matta, Parant, Petlin, Peverelli, Saby, da Silva, Staritsky, Vasarely and Zañartu.

Bb ARTICLES (including less substantial parts of books)

Bb1   Abirached, Robert, 'Sur le roman moderne en France', *Le Français dans le Monde*, 29 (Dec. 64), 6-9.

Bb2   Albérès, R.-M., 'Aux sources du Nouveau Roman: l'impressionnisme anglais', *La Revue de Paris*, 5 (May 62), 74-86.

Bb3   ——, 'L'Ecriture comme art', *Les Nouvelles Littéraires*, 2177 (22.5.69), 5.

Bb4   ——, 'MB et les mythes romanesques', in *Métamorphoses du roman*, Paris: Albin Michel, 1966, pp.[153]-164.

Bb5   ——, 'MB ou le roman transcendental', *La Revue de Paris*, 3 (Mar. 64), 61-71.

Bb6   ——, CR of Aa12, *Les Nouvelles Littéraires*, 1689 (14.1.60), 2.

Bb7   ——, CR of Aa23, *Le Monde*, 7341 (8.8.68), 5.

Bb8   ——, CR of Aa63, Ac19, *Les Nouvelles Littéraires*, 2067 (13.4.67), 5.

Bb9   ——, CR of Aa75, *Les Nouvelles Littéraires*, 2211 (5.2.70), 5.

Bb10   ——, CR of Ba28, *Les Nouvelles Littéraires*, 2137 (5.9.68), 5.

Bb11   ——, CR of Ba28, *Le Français dans le Monde*, 63 (Mar. 69), 55-6.

Bb12   Albert-Levin, Marc, CR of Aa17, *Les Lettres Françaises*, 1178 (13.4.67), 7.

Bb13   Alter, Jean, 'Perspectives et modèles', in *Nouveau Roman hier, aujourd'hui, 1*, ed. Jean Ricardou, Paris: U.G.E., Coll. 10/18, 720, 1972, pp. 35-54 [discussion, pp.55-73].

Bb14   ——, CR of Aa25, *Le Figaro Littéraire*, 631 (24.5.58), 14.

Bb15   ——, CR of Aa63, *French Review*, XLI, 5 (Apr. 68), 757-60.

Bb16   Alyn, Marc, 'Retour au poème', *Le Figaro Littéraire*, 987 (18.3.65), 8.

Bb17   Ames, Van Meter, 'Butor and the Book', *Journal of Aesthetics and Art Criticism* (Baltimore), XXIII, 1 (Fall 64), 159-65.

Bb18* Andrade, Juan, 'Carta de París: De la nueva "literatura objectiva" y de la actitud de la crítica ante las obras teatrales modernas', *La Torre*, VI, 23 (July-Sept. 58), 199-213.

Bb19 André, Robert, 'L'Amérique et l'enfer', *La Nouvelle Revue Française*, 6 (June 62), 1088-93.

Bb20 Angeli, D., CR of Aa67, *Culture Française* (Bari), 8 (1961), 15-17.

Bb21 Aragon, Louis, CR of Aa41, *Les Lettres Françaises*, 922 (12.4.62), 1.

Bb22* Arban, Dominique, CR of Aa20, *France-Observateur*, 345 (20.12.56).

Bb23 Arrouye, J., CR of Aa42, *L'Ecole des Lettres* (17.5.69), 771-2.

Bb24 Ashbery, John, CR of Aa42, *French Review*, XXXII, 1 (Oct. 58), 89-91.

Bb25 Attal, Jean-Pierre, 'Deux détectives littéraires', *Critique*, XVII, 167 (Apr. 61), 319-29.

Bb26 Aubéry, Pierre, 'Le Surréalisme et la littérature actuelle', *Kentucky Romance Quarterly*, XIV (1967), 33-44.

Bb27 Aubral, François, 'Introduction aux lectures de l'œuvre de MB', in Ba3, pp.9-80.

Bb28 —, 'MB et la musique, 1: Présentation', in Ba21, pp.282-3.

Bb29 —, 'Phénomène d'écriture généralisé ou l'oeil machine-à-écrire', in Ba21, pp.224-38 (followed by discussion, pp.239-56).

Bb30 Aury, Dominique, 'La Possession du monde', *La Nouvelle Nouvelle Revue Française*, 71 (Nov. 58), 881-5.

Bb31* Azzoni, Giovanna Terreni, 'Unité et diversité d'un roman contemporain. *La Modification* de MB', in *Studi di letteratura. Storia et filosofia in onore di Bruno Revel*, Florence: Olschki, 1965, pp.573-7.

Bb32 Baqué, Françoise, 'Conquête de nouvelles relations spatio-temporelles', in *Le Nouveau Roman*, Paris: Bordas, 1972, pp.105-12.

Bb33 —, 'Une Tentative de recomposition', *ibid.*, pp.53-64.

Bb34 Barbati, Claudio, 'Un Ingegnere alla ricerca della realtà perduta', *La Fiera Letteraria*, XLI, 43 (3.11.66), 7.

Bb35   Barbéris, Pierre, 'La Chosification', in *Lectures du réel*, Paris: Editions Sociales, 1973, pp.15-17.

Bb36   Barjon, Louis, CR of Aa42, *Etudes*, 296 (Jan. 58), 92-5.

Bb37   Baroche, Christiane, CR of Aa40, *La Nouvelle Revue Française*, 272 (Aug. 75), 89-90.

Bb38   Bars, Henry, 'Des modes littéraires et de la modernité' [Robbe-Grillet, Pinget, MB, Breton], *Revue Générale Belge*, 8 (Aug. 66), 1-17.

Bb39   Barthes, Roland, 'Il n'y a pas d'école Robbe-Grillet', *Arguments* (1958); also in *Essais critiques*, Paris: Seuil, 1964, pp.101-5.

Bb40   ——, 'Littérature et discontinu', *Critique*, XVIII, 185 (Oct. 62), 817-29; also in *Essais critiques*, Paris: Seuil, 1964, pp.175-87.

Bb41   Baumier, Jean, CR of Aa42, *Europe*, 144 (Dec. 57), 149-51.

Bb42   Behar, Jack, 'Old Humanist', *Kenyon Review*, XXXI, 3 (1969), 400-6.

Bb43   Bell, Sheila M., CR of Ba42, *French Studies*, XXXVI, 3 (July 72), 362-3.

Bb44   Belleli, Maria Luisa, CR of Aa20, *Il Mondo*, 33 (17.8.65), 8.

Bb45   Bellour, Raymond, CR of Ba33, *Le Nouvel Observateur*, n.s., 6 (24.12.64), 25.

Bb46*   Berger, Yves, CR of Aa41, *L'Express*, 559 (1.3.62).

Bb47*   Beyer, Jürgen, '*La Modification*' in *Der französische Roman. Vom Mittelalter bis zur Gegenwart*, Düsseldorf: Bagel, 1975, vol. II, pp.298-323.

Bb48   Bigongiari, Pietro, 'La Scrittura di MB o la funzione quantitativa del discorso simbolico', in *La poesia come funzione simbolica del linguaggio*, Milan: Rizzoli, 1972, pp.20-68.

Bb49   Billy, André, 'Gérard Bauer, défenseur des nouveaux romanciers' [MB, Robbe-Grillet, Sarraute], *Le Figaro Littéraire* (6.9.58), 2.

Bb50*   ——, CR of Aa42, *Le Figaro* (6.11.57).

Bb51   Bishop, Tom, 'After that One Great Innovator', *Nation*, CCXV (25.9.72), 249-51.

Bb52 Blanchard, Gérard, 'Le Structuralisme de MB', *Communication et Langages*, 11 (Sept. 71), 5-23.

Bb53 Bloch, Adèle, 'MB and the Myth of Racial Supremacy', *Modern Fiction Studies*, XVI (1970), 57-65.

Bb54 —, CR of Ba4, *Modern Fiction Studies*, XVII, 2 (Summ. 71), 310-11.

Bb55* Bloch-Michel, J., 'Gadgets littéraires', *Preuves*, 178 (Dec. 65), 74-8.

Bb56* —, 'Lettera da Parigi', *Tempo Presente*, V, 4 (Apr. 60), 252-5.

Bb57* Blöcker, Günther, *'Stüfen'*, in *Literatur als Teilhabe*, Berlin, 1966, pp.103-7.

Bb58* Blonski, Jan, 'Czas i zludzenia', [Time and Illusion], *Twórczości*, XIII (1957), 160-1.

Bb59 Boisdeffre, Pierre de, 'L'Expérience de MB', in *Où va le roman?*, Paris: Del Duca, 1972, pp.241-61.

Bb60 —, CR of Aa41, *La Revue de Paris*, 69 (May 62), 168-9.

Bb61 —, CR of Aa42, *La Revue de Paris*, 64 (Dec. 57), 170-1.

Bb62* Bolgár, Mirja, 'Prosan polyfoniaa: MB', in *Rinnakkaiselva. Esseita Ranskan Nykykirjallisuudesta*, Porvoo: Söderström, 1967, pp.81-98.

Bb63 Bonfanti, Giosue, CR of Aa28, *Paragone* (Milan), XII, 140 (Aug. 61), 9-20.

Bb64 Bonfantini, Mario, 'Il "Metodo" di MB', *Il Mondo*, XV, 12 (19.3.63), 13.

Bb65 Bonnefoy, Claude, 'MB: Lectures obliques', *Les Nouvelles Littéraires*, 2391 (23.7.63), 6.

Bb66 —, 'Les Voix de la création', *La Quinzaine Littéraire*, 87 (1.2.70), 14-15.

Bb67 —, CR of Aa32, Aa35, *Les Nouvelles Littéraires*, 2383 (28.5.73), 8.

Bb68 —, CR of Aa40, *Les Nouvelles Littéraires*, 2486 (19.5.75), 4.

Bb69 Borderie, Roger, 'La Grande Sonate pour Hammerklavier', in Ba2, pp.6-11.

Articles

Bb70 —, 'Une Langue 7 fois tournée dáns la bouche', *La Nouvelle Revue Française*, 176 (Aug. 67), 299-305.

Bb71 —, CR of Aa75, *La Quinzaine Littéraire*, 93 (16.4.70), 6.

Bb72 Borel, Jacques, 'Petite introduction à l'*Ulysse* de Joyce' [MB, Robbe-Grillet, Pinget], *Les Temps Modernes* (Jan. 68), 1291-1307.

Bb73* Bosquet, Alain, CR of Aa12, *Combat* (25.2.60).

Bb74 —, CR of Aa31, *Le Monde*, 1077 (12.6.69), 13.

Bb75* —, CR of Aa32, Aa35, *Combat*, 9000 (30.5.73), 7.

Bb76* —, CR of Aa41, *Combat* (6.3.62).

Bb77 —, CR of Aa63, *Combat*, 7170 (3.8.67), 10.

Bb78 —, CR of Aa79, *Combat*, 6623 (7.10.65), 7.

Bb79 Bosseur, Jean-Yves, 'MB et la musique', in *Musique en Jeu*, 4 (1971), 63-111.

Bb80 —, 'MB et la musique, 4: critique, invention et découverte dans *Votre Faust*', in Ba21, pp.316-27 (followed by discussion, pp.328-34).

Bb81 —, 'Les Scènes de foire dans *Votre Faust*', *Obliques*, 4 (1974), 135-47.

Bb82 —, CR of Aa89, *La Quinzaine Littéraire*, 146 (1.8.72), 38.

Bb83 Bougnoux, Daniel, 'Approches de quelques lieux butoriens', in Ba21, pp.345-58 (followed by discussion, pp.359-67).

Bb84 Boulanger, Michel, CR of Aa28, *La Nouvelle Revue Française*, IX, 101 (May 61), 936-8.

Bb85 Bourdet, Denise, 'MB', *La Revue de Paris*, 72 (Nov. 65), 127-33; also in *Encre sympathique*, Paris: Bernard Grasset, 1966, pp.81-91.

Bb86 Bousquet, Robert Edward, 'MB: Le Roman en tant qu'instrument de la transformation du réel', *Diss. Abs.*, XXXI, 6 (Dec. 70), 2905-6A. See Ba5.

Bb87 Boyer, Philippe, CR of Aa69, *Esprit*, 374 (Oct. 68), 428-30.

Bb88 Brabant, O., '*Colloque de Cerisy-Butor*', *Revue Romane*, XI, 1 (1976), 184-9.

Bb89 Brée, Germaine, 'The "New Novel" in France', *American Society of the Legion of Honor Magazine*, XXXI (1960), 33-43.

Bb90   —, 'Novelists in Search of the Novel. The French Scene', *Modern Fiction Studies*, XVI, 1 (Spr. 70), 5-13.

Bb91*   Brenner, Jacques, 'Attention, écoles' [Sartre, Robbe-Grillet, MB], *Cahiers des Saisons*, 17 (Summ. 59), 182-3.

Bb92*   —, CR of Aa41 in *Journal de la vie littéraire, 1962-4*, Paris: Julliard, 1965, pp.9-10.

Bb93   Bronne, Carlo, CR of Aa16, *Marginales* (Brussels), 141-2 (Nov.-Dec. 71), 73.

Bb94   Brooke-Rose, Christine, 'Making it New' [MB, Pinget], *The Observer* (2.10.66), 26.

Bb95   Brooks, Peter, 'In the Laboratory of the Novel', *Daedalus*, 92 (1963), 265-80.

Bb96   Brosman, Catharine Savage, 'A Source and Parallel of MB's *Mobile. In the American Grain*', *Modern Language Review*, LXVI (1971), 315-21.

Bb97   —, 'MB and *Paterson*', *Forum for Modern Language Studies*, VII, 2 (Apr. 71), 126-33.

Bb98   Bruézière, Maurice, 'MB' in *Histoire descriptive de la littérature contemporaine*, vol. I, Paris: Berger-Levrault, 1975, pp.455-66.

Bb99   Bürger, Peter, 'Zeit als Struktur und Schicksal-Versüch über einen Roman von MB', *Neueren Sprachen* (Frankfurt/Main), 6 (June 63), 269-75.

Bb100   Cabanis, José, '*Histoire Extraordinaire*', *Preuves*, 126 (Aug. 61); also in *Plaisirs et Lectures*, Paris: Gallimard, 1964, pp.93-104.

Bb101   Cabau, Jacques, CR of Aa79, *L'Express*, 744 (20.9.65), 60-1; also tr. in *Atlas*, 2 (Feb. 66), 121-5.

Bb102   Cadieu, Martine, CR of Aa89, *Les Lettres Françaises*, 1268 (29.1.69), 27-8.

Bb103*   Cali, Andrea, '*L'Emploi du temps* di MB: un "labirinto" nello spazio e nel tempio', *Annali della Facoltà di Lingue e Letterature Straniere* (Bari), III (1972), 317-33.

Bb104   Campbell, Michael, 'Abroad with a Vengeance' [MB, Rolland], *Time and Tide*, 7 (17.2.61), 257.

Bb105   Camproux, Charles, CR of Aa42, *Les Lettres Françaises*, 717 (10.4.58), 8.

Bb106   Canito, Enrique, 'MB y sus claves', *Insula*, XV, 159 (Feb. 60), 5.

Bb107*   Capote, Truman, CR of Aa41, *New York Times Review of Books* (1.2.63), 14-15.

Bb108   Carduner, J. R., 'The New Novel in France' [Sarraute, Robbe-Grillet, MB], *American Society of the Legion of Honor Magazine*, 1 (1968), 27-34.

Bb109   Carrouges, Michel, CR of Aa42, *La Table Ronde*, 121 (Jan. 58), 138-40.

Bb110   —, CR of Aa57, *Monde Nouveau Paru*, 82 (Oct. 54), 74-7.

Bb111   Carta, Paolo, CR of Aa28, *Il Verri*, 9 (Aug. 63), 128-9.

Bb112   Caruso, Paolo, 'Pour *Mobile*', *L'Arc*, 18 (Apr. 62), 42-8.

Bb113   Chacel, Rosa, CR of Aa42, *Sur*, 266 (Sept.-Oct. 60), 60-8.

Bb114   Chapelan, Maurice, CR of Aa14, *Le Figaro Littéraire*, 817 (18.12.63), 5.

Bb115   —, CR of Ba28, *Le Figaro Littéraire*, 1166 (9.9.68), 18-19.

Bb116*   Chapier, Henri, CR of Aa12, *Synthèses* (Brussels), 163-6 (Dec. 59-Mar. 60), 439-41.

Bb117*   —, CR of Aa28, *Synthèses*, 181-2 (June-July 61), 177-80.

Bb118   Chapsal, Madeleine, CR of Aa12, *L'Express*, 450 (28.1.60), 31.

Bb119   —, CR of Aa23, Aa69, *L'Express*, 872 (4.3.68), 48-9.

Bb120*   —, CR of Aa42, *L'Express*, 332 (31.10.57).

Bb121*   Charbonnier, Georges, CR of Ba1, *Cahiers Littéraires* (5.2.67).

Bb122   Charney, Hanna, 'Quinze Place du Panthéon: La Mythologie du "vérifiable" chez MB', *Symposium*, XIX, 2 (Summ. 65), 125-31.

Bb123*   Chavardès, Maurice, 'Critiques', *Signes du Temps*, 18 (Mar. 65), 24-6.

Bb124   Church, Margaret, Ronald Cummings and John Feaster, 'Five Modern Novelists. A Bibliography' [MB, Camus, Céline, Robbe-Grillet, Sartre], *Modern Fiction Studies*,

XVI, 1 (Spr. 70), 85-100.

Bb125   Cimatti, Pietro, 'I Meccanismi di MB', *La Fiera Letteraria*, 42 (18.10.59), 4.

Bb126   Clarke, Dorothy Clotelle, 'An Hispanic Variation on a French Theme: Mme de Stael, MB, Agudiez', *Symposium*, XXII (1968), 208-14.

Bb127   Claude, Catherine, 'De *Passage de Milan* à *6 810 000 litres d'eau par seconde*. La Forme et l'invention littéraire chez MB', *La Nouvelle Critique*, 17 (Oct. 68), 45-51.

Bb128   Clec'h, Guy le, CR of Aa20, Aa57, *Preuves*, 75 (May 57), 82-4.

Bb129   Clements, Robert J., 'The European Literary Scene', *Saturday Review*, 48 (18.12.65), 29.

Bb130   Cluny, Claude Michel, 'La Planète Mars', in Ba2, pp.36-40.

Bb131   —, CR of Aa22, *La Nouvelle Revue Française*, 203 (Nov. 69), 768-9.

Bb132   Cocking, J. M., 'The *Nouveau Roman* in France' [originally delivered as lecture at Univ. of Western Australia, 26.7.65], *Essays in French Literature*, 2 (Nov. 65), 1-14.

Bb133   Coindreau, M. E., CR of Aa41, *Les Nouvelles Littéraires*, 1801 (8.3.62), 7.

Bb134   Coleman, John, 'Who-done-what?' [MB, Schwarz-Bart], *The Spectator*, 6920 (10.2.61), 197-8.

Bb135   Couffon, Claude, CR of Aa14, *Les Lettres Françaises*, 1008 (19.12.63), 5.

Bb136   Cournot, Michel, 'Bic sans avec' [CR of Ba2], *Le Nouvel Observateur*, 260 (3.9.69), 42-3.

Bb137   Craig, George, CR of Aa33, *Times Literary Supplement*, 3883 (10.9.76), 1127.

Bb138   —, CR of Aa40, *TLS*, 3827 (18.7.75), 791.

Bb139   —, CR of Aa76, *TLS*, 3941 (7.10.77), 1159.

Bb140*   Crevel, L. D. van, CR of Aa30, *Litterair Passpoort*, 193 (Feb. 66), 39-40.

Bb141*   Crickillon, Jacques, 'Tradition et subversion en littérature' [Beckett, MB, Robbe-Grillet, Simon], *Marginales* (Brussels) (Dec. 70), 1-14.

Bb142 Cronel, Hervé, 'MB', *La Nouvelle Revue Française*, 253 (Jan. 74), 97-101.

Bb143 Daix, Pierre, 'Avec MB', *Les Lettres Françaises*, 1037 (9.7.64), 1, 6-7.

Bb144 ——, CR of Aa28, *Les Lettres Françaises*, 868 (23.3.61), 1, 8.

Bb145 Dällenbach, Lucien, 'De pluriel au singulier', in *Les Critiques de notre temps et le nouveau roman*, ed. Réal Ouellet, Paris: Garnier Frères, 1972, pp.146-51; also in Ba8, pp.94-106.

Bb146 Deguise, Pierre, 'MB et le "Nouveau Roman"', *French Review*, XXXV, 2 (Dec. 61), 155-62.

Bb147 Delbouille, P., 'Le "Vous" de *La Modification*', *Cahiers d'Analyse Textuelle*, 5 (1963), 82-7.

Bb148 Delcourt, Xavier, 'Pour MB les frontières entre science-fiction et littérature tendent à s'effacer', *La Quinzaine Littéraire*, 225 (16.1.76), 5-7.

Bb149 ——, 'Volcans et météores', in Ba21, pp.384-98.

Bb150 ——, CR of Aa16, Aa56, *La Quinzaine Littéraire*, 120 (16.6.71), 5-6.

Bb151 ——, CR of Aa76, *La Quinzaine Littéraire*, 244 (16.11.76), 9.

Bb152 ——, CR of Aa84, *La Quinzaine Littéraire*, 143 (16.6.72), 13-14.

Bb153 Delvaille, Bernard, '*Où* de MB ou le voyage organisé', *Combat*, 8455 (23.9.71), 9.

Bb154 Déon, Michel, 'Quand le guide a du génie: la littérature touristique', *Les Nouvelles Littéraires*, 2087 (31.8.67), 1, 8.

Bb155 Desalm, Brigitte, '*Die Stüfen*. Ein Roman von MB', *Sprache im Technischen Zeitalter*, 17-18 (Jan.-June 66), 152-6.

Bb156 Descargues, Pierre, CR of Aa14, *Les Lettres Françaises*, 1006 (5.12.63), 12.

Bb157* ——, CR of Aa79, *Tribune de Lausanne* (10.11.65), 1127.

Bb158   Didier, Béatrice, 'MB et la musique 2: MB et les variations Diabelli', in Ba21, pp.284-91 (followed by discussion, pp.292-8).

Bb159   —, CR of Aa35, *Etudes*, 340 (Feb. 74), 304.

Bb160   —, CR of Ba2, *Le Monde*, 7792 (31.1.70), 11.

BB161   Entry deleted.

Bb162   Dort, Bernard, CR of Aa20, *Les Cahiers du Sud*, 338 (1956), 133-7.

Bb163*   —, CR of Aa57, *France-Observateur*, 208 (10.6.54).

Bb164*   Dousse, Antoine, CR of Aa59, *Revue de Belles-Lettres* (Lausanne), 4 (1968), 55-8.

Bb165*   Dugast, F., CR of Ba31, *Etudes Littéraires*, 1 (Apr. 72), 148-50.

Bb166   Dugorce, Olivier, 'Une Bibliographie généralisée', *Magazine Littéraire*, 110 (Mar. 76), 11-13.

Bb167   Dumazeau, H., 'La Trahison des clercs' [MB, Robbe-Grillet], *Le Français dans le Monde*, 17 (June 63), 2-5.

Bb168*   Dumur, Guy, CR of Aa21, Ba1, *Médecine de France* (May 67).

Bb169*   —, CR of Aa28, *France-Observateur*, 565 (4.3.61).

Bb170*   —, CR of Aa68, *France-Observateur*, 732 (15.5.64).

Bb171   —, CR of Aa79, *Le Nouvel Observateur*, 171 (21.2.68), 33-7.

Bb172   Dupeyron, Georges, 'Montaigne vu par un écrivain d'aujourd'hui', *Bulletin de la Société des Amis de Montaigne*, 3 (July-Sept. 65), 20-5.

Bb173   Dupont, Pierre, CR of Aa79, *Le Figaro*, 7226 (21.11.67), 29.

Bb174*   Durosay, Daniel, 'Il *nouveau roman*: evoluzione e tradizione nel romanzo francese contemporaneo' [MB, Claude Mauriac], *Vita e Pensiero*, XLIV (1961), 476-80.

Bb175   DuVerlie, Claud, CR of Aa35, *Books Abroad*, XLVIII (1974), 324-5.

Bb176   Ehrman, Jacques, CR of Aa12, *French Review*, XXXV, 1 (Oct. 61), 92-3.

Bb177*   Endres, Elisabeth, 'Ortsbeschreibungen', *Der Monat*, 227 (Aug. 67), 72-5.

Bb178   Enzensberger, H. M., 'Aesthetisches Experiment', *Neue Deutsche Hefte*, 53 (Dec. 58), 845-6.

Bb179   Escallier, Emile, 'L'Esprit et la lettre', *Le Nouvel Observateur*, 431 (12.2.73), 67.

Bb180   Fabre-Luce-Karplus, Anne, 'L'Imaginaire dans le nouveau roman ou l'abolition des privilèges', *Revue des Sciences Humaines*, 119 (July-Sept. 65), 441-6.

Bb181   —, 'Du Mouvement en littérature', *Cahiers du XXᵉ Siècle*, I (1973), 7-23.

Bb182   —, CR of Aa32, Aa35, *La Quinzaine Littéraire*, 165 (1.6.73), 7-8.

Bb183   Falbe, A., CR of Ba42, *Rapports*, XLI (1971), 235-8.

Feaster, John, see Bb124.

Bb184   Federman, Raymond, CR of Aa41, *Le Monde* [*des Livres*], 6902 (22.3.67), IV.

Bb185   Field, Trevor, 'Les Anagrammes révélatrices de *L'Emploi du temps*', *Australian Journal of French Studies*, XII (1975), 314-25.

Bb186   —, 'Imagery of Shafts and Tubes in MB's *Passage de Milan*', *Modern Language Review*, LXX, 4 (Oct. 75), 760-3.

Bb187   Fiorlioli, F., CR of Ac19, *Culture Française* (Bari), XIV (1967), 308-9.

Bb188   Fitting, Peter, 'SF Criticism in France' [Vian, MB], *Science-Fiction Studies*, I (1974), 173-81.

Bb189   Flagothier, F., CR of Ba31, *Revue des Langues Vivantes* (Brussels), XXXVII (1971), 636-7.

Bb190   Fleuret, Maurice, CR of Aa89, *Le Nouvel Observateur*, 220 (27.1.69), 44.

Bb191   Fongaro, Antoine, CR of Aa28, *Studi Francesi* (Turin), XVIII (Sept.-Dec. 62), 509-10.

Bb192   —, CR of Ab134, *Studi Francesi*, XII (Jan.-Apr. 68), 191.

Bb193*   Foote, Audrey, CR of Ae4, *Chicago Tribune Book World*, III, 6 (6.2.69), 7.

Bb194   Foucault, Michel, 'Le Langage et l'espace' [Laporte, Le Clézio, Ollier, MB], *Critique*, XX, 203 (Apr. 64), 378-83.

Bb195   Fraser, Ronald, 'MB's "You"', *New Left Review*, 37 (May-June 66), 62-7.

Bb196*   Freustié, Jean, 'Les Chutes du Zambèze', *Adam* (June 67).

Bb197   ——, 'MB: *Portrait de l'artiste en jeune singe*', in *Chroniques d'humeur*, Paris: Mercure de France, 1969, pp.104-9.

Bb198*   Frey, Hans-Jorst, 'Wege des neuen französischen Romans' [MB, Robbe-Grillet, Sarraute], *Schweizer Monatshefte*, XLI (1961), 999-1020.

Bb199   Friedman, Melvin J., 'The Neglect of Time: France's Novel of the Fifties' [Robbe-Grillet, MB, Sarraute, Beckett, Duras, Simon], *Books Abroad*, XXXVI, 2 (Spr. 62), 125-30.

Bb200   Frohock, W. H., 'Faulkner and the *Nouveau Roman*: An Interim Report', *Bucknell Review*, X, 3 (Mar. 62), 186-93.

Bb201   ——, 'Introduction to MB', *Yale French Studies*, 24 (Wint. 60), 54-61.

Bb202   Galey, Matthieu, 'Comment écrit MB', *Arts*, 647 (4.10.57), 4.

Bb203   ——, 'David et Goliath à l'assaut de l'Amérique' [MB, Styron, Updike], *Arts*, 865 (14.3.62), 4.

Bb204   ——, 'Le Nouveau Roman s'amuse', *Arts-Loisirs*, 81 (12.4. 67), 22-3.

Bb205   ——, CR of Aa12, *Arts*, 758 (20.1.60), 4.

Bb206   ——, CR of Aa28, *Arts*, 819 (26.4.61).

Bb207   ——, CR of Aa68, *Arts*, 975 (8.4.64).

Bb208*   Gallego, Julián, 'Crítica', *Revista de Occidente*, XXX, 97 (Apr. 71), 122-4.

Bb209   Gattegno, Felix, 'MB y el "nuevo realismo"', *Ficción*, 13 (May-June 58), 109-11.

Bb210   Gaudier, Jean-Pierre, 'La Chair et le bois: origine classique ou médiévale d'un rêve prévostien?', *Courrier du Centre International d'Etudes Poétiques*, 112 (Mar.-Apr. 76), 10-13.

Bb211   Gaugeard, Jean, CR of Aa63, *Les Lettres Françaises*, 1178 (13.4.67), 6-7.

Bb212   —, CR of Aa68, *Les Lettres Françaises*, 1022 (26.3.64), 4.

Bb213   —, CR of Aa79, *Les Lettres Françaises*, 1102 (30.10. 65), 5.

Bb214*   Gavronsky, Serge, CR of Ae3, *Chicago Tribune Book World*, 47 (23.11.69), 18.

Bb215   Gay-Crosier, Raymond, 'Personnage et pronom personnel dans *La Modification* de MB. Essai sur les modalités de la perspective', in *Le Roman contemporain d'expression française*, ed. Antoine Naaman and Louis Painchaud, Sherbrooke: Univ. Press, 1972, pp.192-217.

Bb216*   —, CR of Aa42, *Neue Zürcher Zeitung*, 49 (31.1.71), 51-2.

Bb217*   Genet, J., 'Letter from Paris', *New Yorker*, 43 (14.12.57), 132-40.

Bb218   Georgin, Robert, 'MB ou les motivations de l'écriture', in *La Structure et le style*, Lausanne: L'Age d'Homme, 1975, pp.49-59.

Bb219   Glicksberg, Charles, 'The Ironic Vision in Modern Literature' [Camus, MB], *Arizona Quarterly*, XX, 4 (Wint. 66), 293-311.

Bb220   Godel, Vahé, CR of Aa76, *Critique*, XXXIII, 360 (May 77), 531-3.

Bb221   Golffing, F., CR of Aa51, *Books Abroad* (Oklahoma), XLV (1971), 67-8.

Bb222   Gorceix, Bernard, 'Littérature et alchimie. Marguerite Yourcenar et MB', in *Sprache, Literatur, Kultur, romanistische Beiträge*, ed. Dietrich Breisemeister, Bern: Lang, 1974, pp.159-70.

Bb223   Graaf, J. de, 'De Mythische Verbeelding in *La Modification* van MB', *Levende Talen*, 225 (1964), 356-66.

Bb224   Grant, Marian A., 'The Function of Myth in the Novels of MB', *A UMLA*, 32 (Nov. 69), 214-22.

Bb225   —, CR of Ba36, *AUMLA*, 43 (May 75), 132-4.

Bb226   Gregarias, Mary, 'MB and William Faulkner: some Structures and Techniques', *Diss. Abs.*, XXX, 2 (Aug. 69), 721A. See Ba11.

Bb227   Gregor, Ulrich, '*Stüfen*', *Neue Deutsche Hefte*, 108 (Nov.-Dec. 65), 148-54.

Bb228   Greidanus, Tine, 'L'Imagination poétique de MB dans *L'Emploi du temps*', *Neophilologus*, L, 3 (July 66), 307-15; 4 (Oct. 66), 422-33.

Bb229*   Grenier, Jean, CR of Aa42, *La Nef* (Dec. 57).

Bb230   Grieve, James, 'Rencontre ou piège: a footnote on *La Modification*', *Australian Journal of French Studies*, VIII, 3 (Sept.-Dec. 71), 314-18.

Bb231   Günther, Helmut, 'MBs Suche nach dem verloren Paradies', *Welt und Wort*, XXI, 7 (July 66), 223.

Bb232   Guth, Paul, CR of Aa42, *Le Figaro Littéraire*, 607 (7.12. 57), 1, 4.

Bb233   Guyard, Marius-François, 'MB', *Etudes*, 298 (Sept. 58), 227-37.

Bb234*   Gysen, René, 'Links en rechts', *Komma*, II (1966), 57-63.

Bb235   Hallier, Jean-Edern, CR of Aa67, *Tel Quel*, 2 (Summ. 60), 57-8.

Bb236*   Hambro, Carl, 'Abstrakt Roman?', *Vinduet*, IV (1958), 285-93.

Bb237   Hammond, Jeannine Lynette, 'MB and the Didactic Novel', *Diss. Abs.*, XXXIV, 7 (Jan. 74), 4621-A. See Ba12.

Bb238   Harbison, Helen M., 'Le Roman contemporain et la musique moderne' [MB, Robbe-Grillet, Queneau], *French Review*, XXXVIII, 4 (Feb. 65), 441-50.

Bb239   Harth, Hélène, 'Der Künstler als Alchemist. Zu MBs *Portrait de l'artiste en jeune singe*', *Germanisch-Romanische Monatschrift* (Heidelberg), XXI (1971), 204-24.

Bb240*   —, CR of Ba31, *Kritikon Litterarum*, 1 (1972), 279-81.

Bb241   Hartung, R., 'Mythologische Abwege', *Neue Deutsche Hefte* (Gütersloh), VII (1960-1), 1030-2.

Bb242   Hassan, Ihab, 'The Avant-garde: Which Way is Forward?' [Beckett, Ionesco, Sarraute, MB, Robbe-Grillet], *The Nation*, CXCIII, 17 (18.11.61), 396-9.

Bb243   Heck, Francis S., *'Ou, le génie du lieu, 2'*, *International Fiction Review*, I, 1 (Jan. 74), 64-5.

Bb244*   Hecquet, Stephen, CR of Aa20, *Bulletin de Paris* (17.1.57).

Bb245   Hedges, Inez Kathleen, 'Temporal and Spatial Structures in Film and the Novel: a Comparison between Ozu Yasujirō's *Kohayagawe-Ke no Aki* and MB's *L'Emploi du temps*', *Diss. Abs.*, XXXVII, 9 (Mar. 77), 5805-A. See Ba13.

Bb246*   Helbo, André, 'Le Groupe dans l'œuvre de MB', *Marginales* (Brussels), 131-2 (May 70), 46-52.

Bb247   ——, 'MB et Henri Pousseur: "Votre Faust"', *Revue Générale Belge* (Brussels), 2 (Feb. 70), 79-90.

Bb248   ——, 'Nouvelle Littérature, nouvel humanisme?', *Synthèses* (Brussels), 286 (Mar. 70), 26-31.

Bb249   ——, *'Portrait de l'artiste en jeune singe* de MB: Une Narration poétique', *Courrier du Centre International d'Etudes Poétiques* (Brussels), 82 (1971), 17-24; also in Ba14, pp.93-9.

Bb250*   ——, 'Rupture et mobilité', *Degrés*, I, 2 (Apr. 73), m/1-m/10.

Bb251*   ——, CR of Aa42, *Le Langage et l'Homme* (Brussels), (1973).

Bb252   Hell, Henri, CR of Aa20, *La Table Ronde*, 111 (Mar. 57), 208-10.

Bb253   Hemmings, John, 'Out of the Brain-Pan', *Listener* (14.8. 69), 222-3.

Bb254*   Hempfer, K. W., CR of Ba31, *Zeitschrift für Französische Sprache und Literatur*, LXXXII (1972), 248-51.

Bb255*   Henriot, Emile, CR of Aa12, Aa67, *Le Monde* (27.1.60).

Bb256*   ——, CR of Aa20, *Le Monde* (20.11.56), 6-7.

Bb257*   ——, CR of Aa42, *Le Monde* (13.11.57), 7.

Bb258 Heppenstall, Rayner, 'The Novels of **MB**', *The London Magazine*, II, 4 (July 62), 57-63.

Bb259 Hitty, Gerold, 'Imaginatio reflexa. A propos du style réflecteur dans *La Modification*', *Vox Romanica* (Bern), XXXIII (1973), 40-59.

Bb260 Hocquette, Hélène, 'Des mots et des chiffres dans *La Modification* de MB', *Vie et Langage*, 243 (June 72), 351-3.

Bb261 Hollier, Denis, CR of Aa30, Ba33, *Mercure de France*, 353 (Apr. 65), 692-9.

Bb262 Horst, Karl August, 'MBs "Modifikation"', *Welt und Wort*, 4 (Apr. 61), 110, 112; also in *Das Spektrum des modernen Romans*, Munich, 1960, pp.133-6.*

Bb263* —, 'Der Philosophische Robinson', *Frankfurter Allgemeine Zeitung* (1.10.60).

Bb264* —, 'Tantalus-früchte' [Sarraute, Robbe-Grillet, MB], *Merkur*, XV, 3 (Mar. 61), 283-7.

Bb265 Houville, Gérard d', CR of Aa42, *La Revue des Deux Mondes* (Dec. 57), 703-5.

Bb266 Howard, Richard, Foreword to Ae4, pp.7-11.

Bb267 Howitt, J. B., 'MB and Manchester', *Nottingham French Studies*, XXI, 2 (Oct. 73), 74-86.

Bb268 Howlett, Jacques, 'Distance et personne', *Esprit*, XXVI, 263-4 (July-Dec. 58), 87-90.

Bb269 —, CR of Aa42, *Les Lettres Nouvelles*, 55 (Dec. 57), 4.

Bb270 Huguenin, Jean-René, 'Le Nouveau Roman se demande s'il a une signification' [Robbe-Grillet, Bloch-Michel, MB], *Arts*, 714 (18.3.59), 3.

Bb271 —, 'Le Roman découvre le monde avec Claude Simon et MB', *Arts*, 699 (3.12.58), 3.

Bb272 —, CR of Aa42, *Arts*, 646 (27.11.57).

Bb273 Ibert, Jean-Claude, 'MB y la literatura experimental', *Insula*, 191 (Oct. 62), 6; in *La Revue Nationale* (Brussels), 349 (Jan. 63), 31-2 under title 'MB et la littérature expérimentale'.

Bb274*   Imbs, Paul, 'Le Temps grammatical français I', in *L'Emploi des temps verbaux en français moderne. Essai de grammaire descriptive*, Paris: Klincksieck, 1968, pp.241-3.

Bb275*   Isou, Isidore, 'Les Pompiers du Nouveau Roman' [Sarraute, Robbe-Grillet, MB], *Les Cahiers de la Créativité* (Paris), [1971].

Bb276*   Jaccottet, Philippe, CR of Aa20, *Gazette de Lausanne* (13.1.57).

Bb277   Jaegar, Patricia J., 'Three Authors in Search of an Elusive Reality: MB, Sarraute, Robbe-Grillet', *Critique. Studies in Modern Fiction*, VI, 3 (Wint. 63-4), 65-81.

Bb278*   Jardin, Claudine, CR of Aa79, *Le Figaro* (14.2.66).

Bb279   Jean, Georges, 'La Poésie de MB', *Le Français Aujourd'hui*, 21 (Mar. 73), 91-5.

Bb280   Jean, Raymond, 'L'Amérique immobile', *Les Cahiers du Sud*, XLIX, 367 (July-Aug. 62), 447-52; also in *La Littérature et le réel. De Diderot au Nouveau Roman*, Paris: Albin Michel, 1965, pp.225-34.

Bb281   ——, 'Mobile, Alabama, U.S.A.', *Europe*, 403-4 (Nov.-Dec. 62), 338-44.

Bb282   ——, CR of Aa12, *Les Cahiers du Sud*, XLVII, 355 (Apr.-May 60), 466-9; also in *La Littérature et le réel. De Diderot au Nouveau Roman*, Paris: Albin Michel, 1965, pp.219-24.

Bb283   ——, CR of Aa14, *Les Lettres Françaises*, 1016 (13.2.64), 7.

Bb284   ——, CR of Aa40, *Le Monde*, 9496 (1.8.75), 9, 10.

Bb285   ——, CR of Aa63, *Le Monde*, 6902 (22.3.67), IV.

Bb286   ——, CR of Aa68, *Les Cahiers du Sud*, LI, 378-9 (July-Oct. 64), 167-8.

Bb287   ——, CR of Aa71, *Les Cahiers du Sud*, L, 371 (Apr.-May 63), 144-5.

Bb288   Jeannet, Angela M., CR of Ae7, *Books Abroad*, XL (1966), 431.

Bb289   ——, CR of Ba34, *ibid.*, 167-8.

Bb290   Jenny, Urs, 'MB oder der Tod des Erzählers', *Merkur* (Stuttgart), 211 (Oct. 65), 992-6.

Bb291 Jolas, Paul, 'MB', *Rencontres Artistiques et Littéraires*, 5 (June 72), 1-10.

Bb292 Josselin, François, CR of Aa57, *Le Nouvel Observateur*, 308 (5.11.70), 40-1.

Bb293 Jouffroy, Alain, CR of Aa63, Ac19, *La Quinzaine Littéraire*, 27 (1.5.67), 5-6.

Bb294* —, CR of Aa68, *L'Express*, 699 (9.4.64).

Bb295 Juin, Hubert, 'La Lecture, pour quoi faire?', *Les Lettres Françaises*, 892 (14.9.61), 4.

Bb296 —, CR of Aa16, Aa56, *Les Lettres Françaises*, 1392 (30.6.71), 6, 7.

Bb297 —, CR of Aa32, Aa35, *Le Monde* [*des livres*] (17.5.73), 17, 19.

Bb298 —, CR of Aa75, *Les Lettres Françaises*, 1319 (28.1.70), 5.

Bb299 —, CR of Aa89, *Les Lettres Françaises*, 902 (23.11.61), 5.

Bb300 Jullian, Philippe, 'Le Renaudot à MB', *Les Nouvelles Littéraires*, 1579 (5.12.57), 1.

Bb301* —, CR of Aa14, *Candide*, 137 (12.12.63).

Bb302 Kanters, Robert, 'Un Œuf dur au bord du Niagara' [CR of production of Aa79], *L'Express*, 870 (19.2.68), 31-2.

Bb303 —, CR of Aa23, *Le Figaro Littéraire*, 1153 (20.5.68), 19-20.

Bb304 —, CR of Aa28, *Le Figaro Littéraire*, 801 (26.4.61), 2.

Bb305 —, CR of Aa32, Aa35, *Le Figaro Littéraire*, 1411 (2.6.73), 16.

Bb306 —, CR of Aa41, *Le Figaro Littéraire*, 828 (3.3.62), 2.

Bb307 —, CR of Aa57, *La Table Ronde*, 81 (Sept. 54), 123-5.

Bb308 —, CR of Aa63, *Le Figaro Littéraire*, 1102 (29.5.67), 19-20.

Bb309 —, CR of Aa68, Ba1, *Le Figaro Littéraire*, 939 (16.4.64), 4.

Bb310 —, CR of Aa79, *Le Figaro Littéraire*, 1017 (14.10.65), 4.

Bb311 Karl, Friedrich R., 'Pursuit of the Real' [Beckett, MB, Robbe-Grillet], *Nation*, CXCIV, 16 (21.4.62), 345-9.

Bb312*   Katanic, Marko, 'Balzac et le Nouveau Roman' [MB, Sarraute, Robbe-Grillet], *Bulletin des Jeunes Romanistes*, 3 (May 61), 21-4.

Bb313*   Kemp, Robert, CR of Aa20, *Les Nouvelles Littéraires*, 1522 (1.11.56).

Bb314*   —, CR of Aa25, *Les Nouvelles Littéraires*, 1618 (4.9. 58).

Bb315*   —, CR of Aa42, *Les Nouvelles Littéraires*, 1577 (21.11. 57).

Bb316   Kempf, Roger, 'Evanston's Keepsake', in Ba2, pp.15-18.

Bb317*   Kesting, Marianne, 'Wort-Symphonie. MBs *Orte*', in *Auf der Suche nach der Realität. Kritische Schriften zur modernen Literatur*, Munich: Piper, 1972, pp.134-7.

Bb318   Klossowski, Pierre, 'Fragments d'une lettre à MB', *Les Cahiers du Chemin*, 1 (15.10.67), 92-100.

Bb319   Knapp, B. L., CR of Ba28, *Books Abroad*, XLIII (1969), 217.

Bb320   Koering, René, 'MB et la musique 3: Une Information: être musicien et collaborer avec MB', in Ba21, pp.299-305 (followed by a discussion, pp.306-15).

Bb321   Kolbert, Jack, 'MB, or a Frenchman goes to New Mexico', *The American Society of the Legion of Honor Magazine*, XLI (1970), 139-54.

Bb322   —, 'Points of View in MB's Criticism: Geometry and Optics', *Kentucky Romance Quarterly*, XVIII (1971), 161-76.

Bb323   —, CR of Aa16, *French Review*, XLV, 4 (Mar. 72), 899-900.

Bb324   —, CR of Aa23, *French Review*, XLII, 4 (Mar. 69), 627-8.

Bb325   —, CR of Aa40, *French Review*, XLIX, 5 (Apr. 76), 822-3.

Bb326   —, CR of Aa51, *French Review*, XLIV, 1 (Oct. 70), 205-7.

Bb327   —, CR of Aa56, *French Review*, XLV, 5 (Apr. 72), 1038-9.

Bb328   —, CR of Aa69, *French Review*, XLII, 2 (Dec. 68), 329-30.

Bb329 —, CR of Aa75, *French Review*, XLV, 1 (Oct. 71), 190-2.

Bb330 —, CR of Aa84, *French Review*, XLVII, 2 (Dec. 73), 487-8.

Bb331 —, CR of Ba36, *French Review*, XLIX, 3 (Feb. 76), 427.

Bb332* Kostelanetz, Richard, 'Dada and the Future of Fiction', *Works*, I, 3 (Spr. 68), 58-66.

Bb333* Krause, G., 'MBs Roman *La Modification*', in *Tendenzen im franz ösische Romanschaffen des XX Jhs*, Frankfurt am Main, 1962, pp.53-67.

Bb334* Krauss, Werner, CR of Ba42, *Deutsche Literatur Zeitung*, XCII, 2 (Feb. 71), 117-18.

Bb335 Kubinyi, Laura R., 'Defense of a Dialogue. MB's *Passing Time*', *Boundary*, 2 (1976), 885-904.

Bb336 Kumm, Karl Ward Graham, 'MB: a Spatial Imagination', *Diss. Abs.*, XXXI, 10 (Apr. 71), 5409-A. See Ba16.

Bb337 Kushnir, Slava M., 'Valery Larbaud, précurseur de MB?', *Revue des Sciences Humaines*, XXXVIII (1973), 291-304.

Bb338 Kustow, Michael, 'New Novelists, New Visions' [MB, Robbe-Grillet, Sarraute, Simon], *Tribune*, 15 (10.4.64), 13.

Bb339* Labbé, L. E., CR of Ba1, *Revista de Literaturas Modernas*, 6 (1967), 136-8.

Bb340 Lacôte, René, CR of Aa2, Aa59, *Les Lettres Françaises*, 1278 (5.3.69), 8.

Bb341 —, CR of Aa84, *Les Lettres Françaises*, 1239 (3.7.68), 10.

Bb342 Laere, François van, 'Les Traducteurs français devant *Finnegans Wake*' [Soupault, MB, du Bouchet], *Revue des Langues Vivantes*, 2 (1968), 126-35.

Bb343* Lagrolet, Jean, 'Nouveau réalisme?' [Blanchot, MB, Robbe-Grillet, Sarraute], *La Nef*, 13 (Jan. 58), 62-70.

Bb344 Lalou, Etienne, CR of Aa63, Ac19, *L'Express*, 827 (24.4. 67), 55-6.

Bb345 —, CR of Aa67, *Les Nouvelles Littéraires*, 1693 (11.2.60), 4.

Bb346* Lalou, René, CR of Aa12, *Les Annales: Conferencia*, 113 (Mar. 60), 35-7.

Bb347 Lambert, Bernard, 'MB fuit son public' [CR of Aa79], *Arts-Loisirs*, 16 (12.1.66), 7.

Bb348 Lanes, Jerrold, CR of Ae1, *Saturday Review*, 42 (24.4. 59), 18-19.

Bb349 Larson, Jeffry, 'The Sibyl and the Iron Floor Heater in MB's *La Modification*', *Papers on Language and Literature*, X, 4 (Aut. 74), 403-14.

Bb350 Lascault, Gilbert, 'L'Egypte des égarements', *Critique*, XXV, 260 (Jan. 69), 54-74.

Bb351* ——, CR of Aa51, *Revue d'Esthétique*, XXIII, 2 (Apr.- June 70), 214-16.

Bb352 ——, CR of Ba2, *La Quinzaine Littéraire*, 85 (15.12.69), 24.

Bb353 Lebeau, Jean, 'De *La Modification* de MB à *La Princesse de Clèves*', *Les Cahiers du Sud*, LVII, 376 (Feb.-Mar. 64), 285-91.

Le Clec'h, see Clec'h.

Bb354 Lecomte, M., 'Richesse de l'investigation critique' [Bataille, Blanchot, MB, Robbe-Grillet], *Synthèses*, 225 (Feb. 65), 74-8.

Bb355 ——, '*Mobile*', *Synthèses*, 190 (Mar. 62), 488-93.

Bb356 Leenhardt, Jacques, 'L'Enjeu politique de l'écriture chez MB', in Ba21, pp.170-84 (followed by discussion, pp.185-202).

Bb357 Leiris, Michel, 'Le Réalisme mythologique de MB', *Critique*, XIV, 129 (Feb. 58), 99-118; also in *Brisées*, Paris: Mercure de France, 1966, pp.215-38; also in *Les Critiques de notre temps et le nouveau roman*, ed. Réal Ouellet, Paris: Garnier, 1972, pp.129-36; also in Aa45, pp.287-312.

Bb358 Lemar, Yves, CR of Aa42, *Arts*, 754 (23.12.59), 3.

Bb359 Lennon, Peter, 'Clouds over the Seine' [MB, Robbe-Grillet], *New York Times Book Review* (8.8.65), 22-3.

Bb360* Lepape, Pierre, CR of Aa63, *Paris-Normandie* (5.5.67).

Bb361*   —, CR of Aa79, *Paris-Normandie* (7.1.66).

Bb362   Lesage, Laurent, 'MB', in *The French New Novel*, University Park, Pennsylvania: Pennsylvania State Univ. Press, 1962, pp.68-77.

Bb363   —, 'Techniques of the Marvellous', *Esprit Créateur*, VI (1966), 34-44.

Bb364   Levitt, Morton P., 'MB: Polyphony or the Voyage of Discovery', *Critique. Studies in Modern Fiction*, XIV (1972), 27-48.

Bb365*   —, CR of Ba36, *Journal of Modern Literature*, IV (1975), 1000-2.

Bb366   L[obet], M[arcel], CR of Aa25, *Revue Générale Belge*, 8 (15.8.58), 138.

Bb367   Lonchampt, Jacques, 'Au Festival de Bruxelles. Portail de "Votre Faust" de MB et Henri Pousseur', *Le Monde*, 6818 (14.12.66), 14.

Bb368   —, 'Création de "Votre Faust" de MB et Henri Pousseur à Milan', *Le Monde*, 7473 (22.1.69), 21.

Bb369*   Loranquin, Albert, CR of Aa12, *Bulletin des Lettres*, 216 (15.3.60), 96-100.

Bb370*   —, CR of Aa20, *Bulletin des Lettres* (15.3.57), 100-1.

Bb371*   —, CR of Aa25, *Bulletin des Lettres* (15.7.58).

Bb372*   —, CR of Aa42, *Bulletin des Lettres*, 193 (15.12.57), 432-3.

Bb373   Luccioni, Gennie, CR of Aa12, Aa67, *Esprit*, XXVII, 284 (May 60), 910-12.

Bb374   Lydon, Mary, 'Sibylline Imagery in MB's *La Modification*', *Modern Language Review*, LXVII, 2 (Apr. 72), 300-8.

Bb375   Lyotard, Jean-François, 'La Confession coupée', in Ba21, pp.124-46 (followed by discussion, pp.147-69).

Bb376*   Macauley, R., 'Letter from Berlin: Poets Black and White' [MB, Césaire], *Encounter*, XXIII (Dec. 64), 52-3.

Bb377   McWilliams, David Dean, 'The Influence of William Faulkner on MB', *Diss. Abs.*, XXXI, 3 (Sept. 70), 1282-A. See Ba18.

Bb378   —, 'The Novelist as Archaeologist: MB's *L'Emploi du temps*', *L'Esprit Créateur*, XV, 3 (Aut. 75), 367-76.

Bb379 —, 'William Faulkner and MB's Novel of Awareness', *Kentucky Romance Quarterly*, XIX (1972), 387-402.

Bb380 Magny, Olivier de, 'Ecriture de l'impossible' [Artaud, Beckett, MB, Michaux], *Lettres Nouvelles*, 32 (Feb. 63), 125-38.

Bb381 —, 'MB ou une géométrie dans le temps', *Monde Nouveau*, 106 (Dec. 56), 99-106.

Bb382 —, 'Panorama d'une nouvelle littérature romanesque', *Esprit*, XVI, 263-4 (July-Aug. 58), 3-17.

Bb383 —, 'Voici dix romanciers [Extracts: Beckett, Cayrol, MB *et al*], *Esprit*, XVI, 263-4 (July-Aug. 58), 19-54.

Bb384 —, CR of Aa12, *Lettres Nouvelles*, 1 (Mar.-Apr. 60), 83-6.

Bb385* —, CR of Aa28, *Lettres Nouvelles*, 13 (Apr. 61).

Bb386 —, CR of Aa42, *Esprit*, XXVI, 257 (Jan. 58), 163-5.

Bb387 Magrini, Liliana, 'MB: Strutture del reale e geometrie celesti', *La Fiera Letteraria*, XL, 33 (29.8.65), 5, 10.

Bb388 Mannoni, O., 'Ce Malentendu universel', *Temps Modernes*, 181 (May 61), 1610-21; also in *Clefs pour l'imaginaire ou l'autre scène*, Paris: Seuil, 1969, pp.263-74.

Bb389 Mansuy, Michel, 'MB: "L'Ecriture pour moi est une colonne vertébrale"', *Travaux de Linguistique et de Littérature* (Strasbourg), VII, 2 (1969), 243-57.

Bb390 Marin, Louis, 'Textes en représentation', *Critique*, XXVI, 282 (Nov. 70), 909-34.

Bb391 Marissel, A., CR of Ba1, *Esprit*, XXXII, 328 (May-June 64), 1204-7.

Bb392 Markow-Totévy, Georges, 'MB', *Bucknell Review*, X, 4 (May 62), 275-91.

Bb393 Martens, Lorna, 'The Diary Novel and Contemporary Fiction: Studies in Max Frisch, MB and Doris Lessing', Ph.D. thesis, Yale Univ., 1976, *Diss. Abs.*, XXXVIII, 1 (July 77), 247-A.

Bb394* Martinoir, Francine de, 'MB ou les textes-personnages', *Sud*, 5-6 (1971), 25-7.

Bb395 Mason, Barbara J., 'An Interpretation through Pattern and Analogy of MB's *Description de San Marco*', *Forum for*

Modern Language Studies, XIV, 1 (Jan. 78), 72-8.

Bb396   Matignon, Renaud, CR of Aa20, *Arts*, 599 (26.12.56).

Bb397   —, CR of Aa68, *Mercure de France*, 1211 (Sept. 64), 145-9.

Bb398   Matignoux, Jean-Louis, CR of Aa28, *Tel Quel*, 7 (Aut. 61), 56-7.

Bb399   Matthews, J. H., 'L'Alchimie et le roman', *Revue des Lettres Modernes*, 94-9 (1964), 51-66.

Bb400*   Maudit, Jean, CR of Aa57, *Témoignage Chrétien* (14.5.54), 2.

Bb401*   Mauriac, Claude, 'L'Inspiration musicale de MB', *Le Figaro* (13.2.69).

Bb402   —, 'Lectures pour finir l'année' [Valéry, MB], *Le Figaro Littéraire*, 610 (28.12.57).

Bb403*   —, 'Literary Letter from France', *New York Times Book Review* (20.4.58), 20-1.

Bb404*   —, 'Literary Letter from France', *New York Times Book Review* (6.11.70), 34.

Bb405   —, 'MB', in *L'Alittérature contemporaine*, Paris: Albin Michel, 1969, pp.235-52.

Bb406*   —, CR of Aa12, *Le Figaro* (13.4.60).

Bb407*   —, CR of Aa20, *Le Figaro* (14.11.57).

Bb408   —, CR of Aa56, *Le Figaro Littéraire*, 1310 (25.6.71), 11.

Bb409   —, CR of Aa63, *Le Figaro*, 7047 (24.4.67), 23.

Bb410*   Maurois, André, CR of Aa20, *Carrefour*, 647 (6.2.57).

Bb411*   —, CR of Aa42, *Carrefour*, 687 (13.11.57).

Bb412   Mayersberg, Paul, 'The Writer as Spaceman', *Listener*, LXX, 1803 (17.10.63), 607-8, 611.

Bb413   Menant Artigas, G., CR of Aa42, in *Des voyages et des livres*, Paris: Hachette, 1973, pp.67-8.

Bb414   Mercier, Vivian, 'James Joyce and the French New Novel', *TriQuarterly*, 8 (Wint. 67), 205-19.

Bb415   —, 'The Schema and the Myth', in *The New Novel. From Queneau to Pinget*, New York: Farrar, Strauss & Giroux, 1971, pp.215-65; also in shorter form in *Mundus Artium*, 3 (Summ. 68), 16-27.

Bb416   Micha, René, 'Sentiment que donne la mosaïque d'Otrante', in Ba2, pp.44-53.

Bb417   Michel, M., CR of Aa79, *Le Monde*, 7116 (29.11.67), 15.

Bb418*   Mielczarek, Elźbieta, 'Le Nouveau Roman devant la critique polonaise', *Romanica Wratislaviensia*, VII (1962), 71-86.

Bb419*   Miguel, A., CR of Aa63, *Beaux-Arts* (22.4.67).

Bb420   Miller, J. Hillis, 'The Anonymous Walkers' [Beckett, MB, Cayrol, Duras, Robbe-Grillet, Sarraute, Simon], *Nation*, CXC, 17 (23.4.60), 351-4.

Bb421   Milner, Max, CR of Ba31, *Information Littéraire*, 3 (May-June 72), 27-8.

Bb422   Minogue, Valerie, 'Distortion and Creativity in the Subjective Viewpoint', *Forum for Modern Language Studies*, XII, 1 (Jan. 76), 37-49.

Bb423   Molnar, Thomas, 'The New French School of Object-Worshippers' [Robbe-Grillet, MB], *The Catholic World*, 123 (Oct. 58), 31-5.

Bb424   Mombello, G., CR of Ab200, *Studi Francesi*, L (1973), 327.

Bb425*   Montal, R., CR of Aa42, *Le Thyrse* (Brussels), LX (1958), 256-7.

Bb426   Morrissette, Bruce, 'International Aspects of the *Nouveau Roman*', *Contemporary Literature*, XI (1970), 155-68.

Bb427   —, 'Narrative "You" in Contemporary Literature', *Comparative Literature Studies*, II (1965), 1-25.

Bb428   —, 'The New Novel in France', *Chicago Review*, XV, 3 (Wint.-Spr. 62), 1-19.

Bb429*   Nadeau, Maurice, CR of Aa28, *L'Express*, 511 (30.3.61).

Bb430   Nahnybida, Oksanna, 'From Mythology to Mythopoesis. Mythological Figures and Patterns in the Novels of MB', *Diss. Abs.*, XXXII, 7 (Jan. 72), 4012-A. See Ba22.

Bb431   Nathan, Monique, 'Un Roman expérimental', *Critique*, XIII, 116 (Jan. 57), 17-21.

Bb432   Naudin, Marie, CR of Aa63, *French Review*, XLI, 4 (Feb. 68), 584-5.

Bb433* Niel, Mathilde, 'L'Echec de l'amour' [Mauriac, Sagan, MB], *Synthèses* (Brussels), 181-2 (June-July 61), 37-67.

Bb434* Nourissier, François, CR of Aa12, Aa67, *France-Observateur*, 509 (4.2.60).

Bb435 Nye, Robert, 'Lying near the Truth', *Guardian* (12.5.67), 8.

Bb436 O'Brien, Justin, CR of Ae1, *New York Times Book Review* (29.3.59), 4, 33; also in *The French Literary Horizon*, New Brunswick, New Jersey: Rutgers Univ. Press, 1967, pp.329-30.

Bb437 O'Donnell, Thomas D., 'Joycean Themes and Techniques in the Works of MB', *Diss. Abs.*, XXXII, 6 (Dec. 71), 3321-A. See Ba23.

Bb438 —, 'MB and the Tradition of Alchemy', *International Fiction Review*, II, 2 (July 75), 150-3.

Bb439 —, 'Polemic', *Diacritics*, II, 2 (Summ. 72), 52-6.

Bb440 O'Flaherty, Kathleen, 'MB', in *The Novel in France, 1945-65. A General Survey*, Cork: Univ. Press, 1973, pp.129-44.

Bb441 Olmi, Massimo, 'Butor alla *N.R.F.*?', *Fiera Letteraria*, XLI, 11 (24.3.66), 21.

Bb442 O'Neill, Kathleen, 'On *Passing Time*', *Mosaic*, 1 (Aut. 74), 29-33 (followed by MB's response, pp.33-4).

Bb443 Opitz, Kurt, 'The Reality of the Continental Novel', [MB, Robbe-Grillet, Sarraute], *Modern Language Journal*, L, 2 (Feb. 66), 84-91.

Bb444 Ormesson, Jean d', CR of Aa16, Aa56, *Les Nouvelles Littéraires*, 2280 (4.6.71), 6.

Bb445 Ortzen, Len, 'Recent French Novelists' [Cayrol, MB, Queneau, Sagan], *Twentieth Century*, 994 (Dec. 59), 462-70.

Bb446* Oster, Daniel, CR of Aa63, Ac19, *La Gazette de Lausanne* (6.5.67).

Bb447 Otten, Anna, CR of Ba21, *Books Abroad*, XLVII, 1 (Wint. 74), 46-51.

Bb448   Ouellet, Réal, 'MB', in *Les Critiques de notre temps et le nouveau roman*, Paris: Garnier, 1972, pp.128-9.

Bb449   Paci, Enzo, 'Nota su Robbe-Grillet, MB e la fenomenologia', *Aut Aut*, 69 (May 62), 234-7.

Bb450*   Pack, Claus, CR of Aa41, *Wort und Wahrheit* (Freiburg), 222 (Feb. 67), 141-2.

Bb451*   Palante, Alain, CR of Aa14, *France-Catholique* (15.5.64).

Bb452*   —, CR of Aa42, *France-Catholique* (13.12.57).

Bb453   Paris, Jean, 'The New French Generation', *American Society of the Legion of Honor Magazine*, XXI (1960), 45-51.

Bb454   Passias, Katharine, 'Structure and Movement in Three French New Novels, 1957-62. A Deep and a Surface Comparison', *Diss. Abs.*, XXXV, 11 (May 75), 7265-A. See Ba25.

Bb455   Patai, Daphne, 'Temporal Structure as Fictional Category in MB's *La Modification*', *French Review*, XLVI, 6 (May 73), 1117-28.

Bb456   Pautasso, Sergio, 'MB fra critica e romanzo', *Aut Aut*, 69 (May 62), 230-3.

Bb457   —, 'Repertorio critico di MB', *L'Europa Letteraria*, 30-2 (July-Sept. 64), 203-5.

Bb458*   Pérez Minik, Domingo, '*La modificación* de MB', in *La novela extranjera en España*, Madrid: Josefina Betancor, 1973, pp.33-8.

Bb459*   —, 'La novela extranjera en España: Uwe Johnson, MB', *Insula*, XXXV, 279 (Feb. 70), 7.

Bb460   Perrone-Moisés, Leyla, 'Comment les Brésiliens ont dévoré MB', in Ba21, pp.368-73 (followed by discussion, pp.374-83).

Bb461   —, CR of Aa70, *La Quinzaine Littéraire*, 193 (1.9.74), 13-14.

Bb462   Perros, Georges, 'En guise de salut', *Les Cahiers du Chemin*, 17 (15.1.73), 218-21; also in *Papiers collés 2*, Paris: Gallimard, 1973, pp.354-8; also in Ba3, pp.5-8.

Bb463   —, 'La Pointe du Raz', in Ba2, pp.24-31.

Bb464   —, 'Pour MB', *La Nouvelle Revue Française*, 91 (1.7.60), 160-3.

Bb465   —, CR of Aa20, *La Nouvelle Nouvelle Revue Française*, 48 (1.12.56), 1095-7.

Bb466   —, CR of Aa57, *La Nouvelle Nouvelle Revue Française*, 20 (1.8.54), 316-17.

Bb467   Pfeiffer, Jean, 'Le Livre et ses significations', *Revue d'Esthétique*, XVIII (1965), 95-7.

Bb468   —, 'La Marchesa de Goya', in Ba2, pp.56-9.

Bb469*   —, CR of Aa31, *Marginales* (Brussels), 129 (Nov. 69), 53-5.

Bb470   'Le Livre qui n'est à personne (itinéraire de MB)', *Synthèses* (Brussels), 210-1 (Nov.-Dec. 63), 152-7.

Bb471*   Pia, Pascal, CR of Aa25, *Carrefour*, 725 (6.8.58).

Bb472*   —, CR of Aa67, *Carrefour*, 804 (10.2.60), 20.

Bb473   Piatier, Jacqueline, 'Critique romanesque, alchimiste et anthropophage', *Le Monde* [*des Livres*], 1279 (26.4.73), 12.

Bb474   —, 'MB devant ses juges', *Le Monde*, 8737 (15.2.73), 17-18.

Bb475   —, 'Le Nouveau Roman: MB', *Tendances*, 48 (Aug. 67), 400-2.

Bb476   —, CR of Aa14, *Le Monde (hebdomadaire)*, 790 (5.12. 63), 10.

Bb477   —, CR of Aa16, Aa56, *Le Monde*, 8249 (23.7.71), 9.

Bb478   —, CR of Aa51, *Le Monde*, 7792 (31.1.70), 1.

Bb479   —, CR of Aa70, *Le Monde (hebdomadaire)*, 1349 (29.8. 74), 12.

Bb480   —, CR of Aa84, *Le Monde*, 9607 (12.12.75), 19, 25.

Bb481   —, CR of parts of Ab159, *Le Monde*, 6187 (5.12.64), 12.

Bb482   —, CR of Ba31, *Le Monde*, 8125 (26.2.71), 15.

Bb483   Picon, G., CR of Aa42, *Mercure de France*, 1113 (Jan. 58), 86-90; also in *L'Usage de la lecture*, Paris: Mercure, 1961, pp.265-70.

Bb484   Piel, Jean, CR of Aa25, *Critique*, XII, 141 (Feb. 59), 182-4.

Bb485   Pierre, Rolland, CR of Aa63, *La Nouvelle Critique*, 18 (Oct. 68), 50-5.

Bb486   Pingaud, Bernard, CR of Aa20, *Les Lettres Nouvelles*, 43 (Nov. 56), 646-8.

Bb487   —, CR of Aa42, *Esprit*, XXVI, 2 (1958), 91-9.

Bb488*   Pires, A., 'MB e Robbe-Grillet', *Brotéria* (Lisbon), LXXIV (1962), 87-94.

Bb489*   Pollman, Leo, 'MB: *La Modification*', in *Der französische Roman*, Berlin, 1968, pp.294-309.

Bb490   Poole, Roger, 'Objectivity and Subjectivity in the *Nouveau Roman*', *20th Century Studies*, 6 (Dec. 71), 41-52.

Bb491   Pouillon, Jean, 'A Propos de *La Modification*', *Les Temps Modernes*, 142 (1957-8), 1099-1105.

Bb492   —, 'Les Règles du je' [MB, Lagrolet, Sarraute], *Les Temps Modernes*, 134 (Apr. 57), 1591-8.

Bb493*   Poulet, Robert, CR of Aa12, *Rivarol* (11.3.60).

Bb494   Pousseur, Henri, 'La Foire de "Votre Faust"', *Marche Romane*, XX (1970), 21-37.

Bb495   —, 'Life Electronic Music', in Ba2, pp.80-5.

Bb496   Prasteau, Jean, 'Chronique d'une ascension', *Le Figaro Littéraire*, 1223 (27.10.69), 8.

Bb497   Prince, Martin, CR of Ae1, *Yale Review*, XLVIII, 4 (June 59), 598-9.

Bb498   Pugh, Anthony R., 'MB on Beethoven, or the limits of Formalism', *International Fiction Review*, III, 1 (Jan. 76), 65-9.

Bb499   Puputti, Leena, 'Le Démonstratif, signe de la prise de conscience dans *La Modification* de MB', *Neophilologische Mitteilungen*, LXVII (1966), 144-55.

Bb500   Quenelle, G., 'Une Présentation de *La Modification* de MB', *Le Français dans le Monde*, 5 (Dec. 61), 42-8.

Bb501   Quéréel, Patrice, '*Passage de Milan*, description d'une topique', in Ba21, pp.70-80 (followed by discussion, pp.81-90).

Bb502   Raban, Jonathan, CR of Ae4, *New Statesman*, 2041 (24.4.70), 585.

Bb503   Raillard, Georges, ' "le butor étoilé ATTENTION"! Heptaèdre', in Ba21, pp.399-432 (followed by discussion, pp.433-4).

Bb504   —, 'Le Carnaval de Rio', in Ba2, pp.68-75.

Bb505   —, 'Clés pour le "nouveau roman" ', *Le Français dans le Monde*, 17 (June 63), 20-1.

Bb506   —, 'MB', in *Ecrivains d'aujourd'hui 1940-1960. Dictionnaire anthologique et critique*, ed. Bernard Pingaud, Paris: Grasset, 1960, pp.145-57.

Bb507   —, 'MB', *Livres de France*, XXXI, 6 (June-July 63), 2-5, 15.

Bb508   —, 'Ouverture', in Ba21, pp.11-15.

Bb509   —, 'Peindre une vague', in Aa52, pp.9-16.

Bb510   —, 'De quelques éléments baroques dans le roman de MB', *Cahiers de l'Association Internationale des Etudes Françaises*, 14 (Mar. 62), 179-94.

Bb511   —, 'Quelques notes prises au cours d'un premier déchiffrement de *Où, le génie du lieu, 2*', *Marche Romane*, XXI (1971), 41-55.

Bb512   —, 'Référence plastique et discours littéraire chez MB', *Critique*, XXVIII, 299 (Apr. 72), 328-44; also in *Nouveau Roman hier, aujourd'hui, 2*, ed. Jean Ricardou, Paris: U.G.E., Coll. 10/18, 725, 1972, pp. 255-78 (followed by discussion, pp.279-95).

Bb513   —, 'Le Temple-livre', in Aa21, pp.443-502; also in Ba28, pp.75-145.

Bb514   —, CR of Aa33, *Le Nouvel Observateur*, 2519 (12.2.76), 6.

Bb515   —, CR of Aa40, *La Quinzaine Littéraire*, 209 (15.4.75), 14-16.

Bb516   —, CR of Aa68, *Le Français dans le Monde*, 28 (Oct.-Nov. 64), 22-3.

Bb517   —, CR of Ba3, *Le Français dans le Monde*, 104 (Apr.-May 74), 53.

Bb518   Rambures, J. L. de. 'MB: Présentation', *Réalités*, 267 (Apr. 68), 117.

Bb519*   Rattaud, Janine, 'MB', *Praxis des Neusprachlichen Unterrichts* (Dortmund), 15 (1968), 286-8.

Bb520*   Rebatet, Lucien, CR of Aa42, *Dimanche-Matin* (24.11.57).

Bb521   Recht, Roland, 'Le Point privilégié', *La Nouvelle Revue Française*, 141 (Sept. 64), 504-9.

Bb522   Reck, Rima Drell, 'Old and New in the French New Novel', *The Southern Review*, I, 4 (Aut. 65), 791-802.

Bb523   Réda, Jacques, CR of Aa31, *La Nouvelle Revue Française*, XVII, 204 (Dec. 69), 887-9.

Bb524   Ricardou, Jean, 'L'Histoire dans l'histoire', *Critique*, XXII, 231-2 (Aug.-Sept. 66), 711-29.

Bb525   ——, 'MB ou le roman et ses degrés', *La Nouvelle Revue Française*, 90 (1.6.60), 1157-61.

Bb526   Rice, Donald, 'Etude critique des romans de MB', *Diss. Abs.*, XXXI, 1 (July 70), 401-A. See Ba29.

Bb527   ——, 'The Exploration of Space in MB's *Où*', *Twentieth Century Fiction. Essays for Germaine Brée*, ed. George Stambolian, New Brunswick, New Jersey: Rutgers Univ. Press, 1975, pp.198-222.

Bb528   Ridder, A. de, 'Die nieuwe franse roman. MB', *De Vlaamse Gids* (Brussels), XLIV (1960), 355-77.

Bb529   Rigolot, François, CR of Aa65, *French Review*, XLVIII, 2 (Dec. 74), 411-12.

Bb530   Rinaldi, Angelo, CR of Aa40, *L'Express*, 1244 (12.6.75), 68-9.

Bb531   Rogers, W. S., 'An Essay in Avant-Garde Writing', *Saturday Review* (17.2.62), 31.

Bb532*   Rossi, Aldo, 'Il punto sull'attualità in Francia', *Paragone*, XI, 124 (Apr. 60).

Bb533   Rossum-Guyon, Françoise van, 'Aventures de la citation chez MB', in Ba21, pp.17-39 (followed by discussion, pp.40-54).

Bb534*   ——, '*Le Génie du lieu* ou quelques aspects des dernières œuvres de MB', *Het Franse Boek* (Amsterdam), XXXVI (1966), 156-62.

Bb535   —, 'MB. Le Roman comme instrument de connaissance', in *Positions et Oppositions sur le roman contemporain. Actes du colloque organisé par le centre de philologie et littérature romanes de Strasbourg (avril 1970)*, ed. Michel Mansuy, Paris: Klincksieck, 1970, pp.163-74 (followed by discussion, pp.175-80).

Bb536   —, CR of Aa42, in *Les Critiques de notre temps et le nouveau roman,* ed. Réal Ouellet, Paris: Garnier, 1972, pp.136-40.

Bb537   Roudaut, Jean, 'Il Campidoglio', in Ba2, pp.91-9.

Bb538   —, 'Contribution d'histoire littéraire sur la légende du grand veneur', *Magazine Littéraire*, 110 (Mar. 76), 16.

  —, 'L'Effort d'imaginer', see Bb545.

Bb539   —, 'La Littérature et les nombres', *Critique*, XXVII, 284 (Jan. 71), 26-44.

Bb540   —, 'Mallarmé et MB. A Gossip', *Cahiers du Sud*, LVIII, 378-9 (July-Oct. 64), 29-33.

Bb541   —, 'MB-Borges', *Magazine Littéraire*, 110 (Mar. 76), 12.

Bb542   —, 'MB, critique', *Critique*, XVI, 158 (July 60), 579-90.

Bb543   —, '*Mobile*: Une lecture possible', *Les Temps Modernes*, 198 (Nov. 62), 884-96.

Bb544   —, 'Parenthèse sur la place occupée par l'étude intitulée *6 810 000 litres d'eau par seconde* parmi les autres ouvrages de **MB**', *La Nouvelle Revue Française*, 165 (Sept. 66), 498-509.

Bb545   —, 'Répétition et modification dans deux romans de **MB**', *Saggi e Ricerche di Letteratura Francese*, VIII (1967), 309-24; also extract under title 'L'Effort d'imaginer', in *Les Critiques de notre temps et le nouveau roman*, ed. Réal Ouellet, Paris: Garnier, 1972, pp.144-6.

Bb546   —, CR of Aa33, *Le Monde*, 9678 (5.3.76), 15.

Bb547   Roudiez, Leon S., 'Aspects de la production du sens dans *Où*', in Ba21, pp.257-72 (followed by discussion, pp.273-8).

Bb548   —, 'Une gaieté violette', *Romanic Review*, LXVIII (1977), 32-42.

Bb549   —, 'Gloses sur les premières pages de *Mobile* de MB', *Modern Language Notes*, LXXXV, 6 (Nov. 72), 83-95.

Bb550   —, *'Illustrations II'*, *Books Abroad*, XLVII, 1 (Wint. 73), 26-35.

Bb551   —, 'MB', in *French Fiction Today. A New Direction*, New Brunswick, New Jersey: Rutgers Univ. Press, 1972, pp.278-315.

Bb552   —, 'MB. "Du Pain sur la planche"', *Critique*, XX, 209 (Oct. 64), 851-62.

Bb553   —, 'Problems of Point of View in the Early Fiction of MB', *Kentucky Romance Quarterly*, XVIII, 2 (Apr. 71), 145-59.

Bb554   —, CR of Aa79, *French Review*, XXXIX, 4 (Feb. 66), 667-8.

Bb555   —, CR of Aa89, *French Review*, XLVIII, 4 (Mar. 75), 793-4.

Bb556   —, CR of Ae2, *New York Times Book Review* (17.10.61), 7, 16.

Bb557   —, CR of Ba31, *Romanic Review*, LXIII, 1 (Feb. 72), 76-80.

Bb558   Rousseaux, A., 'Après les prix', *Le Figaro Littéraire*, 555 (8.12.56), 2.

Bb559   —, 'Ressources et limites de MB', in *Littérature du XXe siècle*, VII, Paris: Albin Michel, 1961, pp.124-52.

Bb560   —, CR of Aa12, Aa67, *Le Figaro Littéraire*, 718, (23.1. 60), 2.

Bb561   —, CR of Aa42, *Le Figaro Littéraire*, 602 (2.11.57), 2.

Bb562   —, CR of Aa42, *Le Figaro Littéraire*, 626 (19.4.58), 2.

Bb563   Rousset, Jean, 'Trois Romans de la mémoire' [MB, Simon, Pinget], *Cahiers Internationaux de Symbolisme*, 9-10 (1965-6), 75-85; also in *Les Critiques de notre temps et le nouveau roman*, ed. Réal Ouellet, Paris: Garnier, 1972, pp.27-35.

Bb564   Roy, Claude, 'Un Athlète complet', *Le Nouvel Observateur*, 174 (13.3.68), 34-5.

Bb565*   —, 'De la musique avant toute chose', *Le Nouvel Observateur* (12.5.69), 38-9.

Bb566   Ruff, Marcel A., 'Un Nouveau Roman du temps et du lieu', *L'Arc*, 5 (Wint. 59), 41-4.

Bb567*   Rupolo, Wanda, 'Le ragioni narrative di **MB**', *Nuova Antologia* (Rome) (1976), 234-45.

Bb568   Ryan, Marie-Laure, 'Le narrateur et son texte dans *L'Emploi du temps* de **MB**', *Rocky Mountain Review of Language and Literature*, XXX, 1 (Wint. 76), 27-40.

Bb569   Sábato, Ernesto, 'Algunas reflexiones a propósito del *nouveau roman*', *Sur*, 285 (Nov.-Dec. 63), 42-67.

Bb570*   Sabbe, Herman, 'Literatuuren musiek verenigd in theorie en praktijk. Het Contemporain geval MB-Henri Pousseur, "Invitation à l'utopie"', *Nieuw Vlaams Tijdschrift*, XXIX (1976), 366-99, 797-816.

Bb571   St Aubyn, F. C., 'MB and Phenomenological Realism', *Studi Francesi*, 16 (Jan.-Apr. 62), 51-62.

Bb572   —, 'MB. A Bibliography of his Works 1945-1972', *West Coast Review* (June 1977), 43-9.

Bb573   —, 'MB et le bouddhisme. L'Exemple de "Dans les flammes"', in Ba21, pp.335-9 (followed by discussion, pp.340-4).

Bb574   —, 'MB's America', *Kentucky Foreign Language Quarterly*, XI, 1 (1964), 40-8.

Bb575   —, CR of Aa35, *French Review*, XLVIII (1974-5), 1060-1.

Bb576   St Pierre, Gaëtan, 'Point de vue narratif et technique de la "coïncidence" dans deux romans de **MB**', *Liberté*, XII, 1 (Jan.-Feb. 70), 99-108.

Bb577   Saisselin, Remy G., CR of Aa67, *Journal of Aesthetics and Art Criticism*, XIX (1961), 484-5.

Bb578   Sanguinetti, Edoardo, 'MB. "Une machine mentale"', *Il Verri*, III, 2 (Apr. 59), 42-55; also in *Il Novecento letterario francese attraverso la critica italiana*, Naples, 1971, pp.157-66.

Bb579*   Scheffel, H., 'Den Abstand verringern zwischen Welt und Literatur. Besuch bei MB', *Frankfurter Allgemeine Zeitung*, 126 (12.6.76).

Bb580*   —, CR of Aa20, *Der Monat*, 146 (Nov. 60), 76-83.

Bb581   Schifres, Alain, 'Littérature-laboratoire' [MB, Queneau, Saporta], *Réalités*, 270 (July 68), 92-5.

Bb582   Sellier, Philippe, 'Fonction du mythe dans *L'Age d'homme* (Leiris) et dans *L'Emploi du temps* (MB)', *Mosaic*, IX, 1 (Aut. 75), 143-56.

Bb583*   Selva, Marcio de la, 'MB. *Sobre literatura II*', *Cuadernos Americanos*, CLX, 5 (Sept.-Oct. 68), 286-7.

Bb584   Senart, Philippe, 'MB', in *Chemins Critiques*, Paris: Plon, 1966, pp.33-8.

Bb585   —, CR of Aa12, *Mercure de France*, 1161 (May 60), 102-6.

Bb586   —, CR of Aa20, *Arts*, 602 (16.1.57), 5.

Bb587   —, CR of Aa41, *Mercure de France*, 1186 (June 62), 312-13.

Bb588*   —, CR of Aa68, *Combat*, 6270 (20.8.64), 7.

Bb589   Serval, Bernard, CR of Aa57, *La Vie Intellectuelle*, XXV (Oct. 54), 114.

Bb590   Seylaz, J.-L., 'La Tentative romanesque de MB de *L'Emploi du temps* à *Degrés*', *Etudes de Lettres* (Lausanne), III, 4 (Oct.-Dec. 60), 209-21.

Bb591   Sicard, Michel, 'De *Don Juan* de MB', *Obliques*, 5 (1974), 86-98.

Bb592   —, 'MB, *Don Juan*', *Critique*, XXX, 326 (July 74), 640-65.

Bb593   —, 'MB, esquisse pour un portrait explosé', *Magazine Littéraire*, 110 (Mar. 76), 9-10.

Bb594   Simon, John K., 'Perception and Metaphor in the New Novel: Notes on Robbe-Grillet, Claude Simon and MB', *TriQuarterly*, 4 (Aut. 64), 153-82.

Bb595   —, 'View from the Train: MB, Gide, Larbaud', *French Review*, XXXVI, 2 (Dec. 62), 161-6.

Bb596   Simon, Pierre-Henri, 'Festival MB', *Le Monde* [*des Livres*], 7356 (7.9.68), I.

Bb597*   —, CR of Aa42, *Le Monde* (7.3.62); also in *Diagnostic* *des lettres françaises contemporaines*, Brussels: La Renaissance du Livre, 1966, pp.312-14.*

Bb598* —, CR of Aa68, Ba1, *Le Monde* [*des Livres*] (23.4.64), 10.

Bb599* Sion, Georges, 'Les Quatre prix de fin d'année' [MB, Mégret, Guimard, Vailland], *Revue Générale Belge*, 12 (Dec. 57), 48-50.

Bb600 Smith, Esther Young, 'Crisis in the Novel: Max Frisch and MB', *Diss. Abs.*, XXXVII, 3 (Sept. 76), 2171-A. See Ba35.

Bb601 Smock, Ann, 'The Disclosure of Difference in MB', *Modern Language Notes*, LXXXIX, 4 (May 74), 654-68.

Bb602* Specovius, Günther, 'Der "objective Roman" ist nicht objectiv', *Deutsche Rundschau*, LXXXVI, 10 (Oct. 60), 940-4.

Bb603 Spencer, M. C., 'Architecture and Poetry in *Réseau Aérien*', *Modern Language Review*, LXIII, 1 (Jan. 68), 57-65.

Bb604 —, 'Avatars du mythe chez Robbe-Grillet et MB: Etude comparative de *Projet pour une révolution à New York* et de *Mobile*', in *Colloque de Cerisy: Robbe-Grillet*, Vol. 1, ed. Jean Ricardou, Paris: U.G.E., Coll. 10/18, 1079, 1967, pp. 64-84 (followed by discussion, pp. 85-107).

Bb605 —, 'Etat présent of MB studies', *Australian Journal of French Studies*, VIII, 1 (Jan.-Apr. 71), 84-97.

Bb606 —, 'Literature in an Electronic Age', *Meanjin Quarterly*, XXVIII, 119 (Dec. 69), 472-8.

Bb607 —, 'MB et Fourier', in Ba21, pp.203-14 (followed by discussion, pp.215-23).

Bb608 —, 'MB since 1960', in *Australian Universities Language and Literature Association, 1969* (Proceedings and Papers on the Twelfth Congress held at the University of Western Australia, 5-11 Feb. 69), ed. A. P. Treweek, pp.293-4.

Bb609* —, 'L'Ouverture chez MB', *Degrés*, I, 1 (Jan. 73), 1/1-1/15.

Bb610 —, '*Son et lumière* at Niagara Falls', *Australian Journal of French Studies*, VI, 1 (Jan.-Apr. 69), 101-12.

Bb611 —, 'The Unfinished Cathedral. MB's *L'Emploi du temps*', *Essays in French Literature*, 6 (Nov. 69), 81-101.

Bb612   Spitzer, Leo, 'Quelques aspects de la technique des romans de MB', *Archivum Linguisticum*, XIII (1961), 171-95; XIV (1962), 49-76; also in *Etudes de Style*, Paris: Gallimard, 1970, pp.482-531.

Bb613   Stakenburg, J., 'Robbe-Grillet, MB', *Streven*, XIII (1959-60), 227-35.

Bb614   Stanton, D. C., CR of Ba8, *Books Abroad*, XLVII (1973), 513-4.

Bb615   Steens, M. J., 'Le Grand Schisme de MB', *Revue des Sciences Humaines*, 134 (Apr.-June 69), 331-7.

Bb616   ——, 'La Vision chez MB', *Neophilologus*, LIII, 1 (Jan. 69), 8-10.

Bb617*   Stefanescu, Cornelia, '*Répertoire*, meditatie aspura artei romanului', in Domingo Pérez Minik, *La novela extranjera en España*, Madrid: Josefina Betancor, 1973, pp.295-326.

Bb618   Steinberg, Günter, 'Zum erlebten Rede in MB's *La Modification*', *Vox Romanica* (Bern), XX (1972), 334-64.

Bb619   Sturrock, John, Introduction to Aa49.

Bb620   ——, 'MB', in *The French New Novel*, London: Oxford Univ. Press, 1969, pp.104-69.

Bb621   ——, CR of Ae6, *New York Times Book Review* (28.12. 69), 10, 12, 13.

Bb622   ——, CR of Ba31, *French Studies*, XXVII, 3 (July 73), 367-9.

Bb623   ——, CR of Ba36, *French Studies*, XXIX, 3 (July 75), 371-2.

Bb624   Suckling, Norman, CR of Aa16, *French Studies*, VII, 4 (Oct. 73), 485-6.

Bb625   Suleiman, Susan, CR of Ba31, *French Review*, XLV, 5 (Apr. 72), 1049-50.

Bb626   Tadié, J. Y., CR of Ba31, *La Nouvelle Revue Française*, 227 (Nov. 71), 97-8.

Bb627*   Tamada, Kenji, 'Une Etude sur *Passage de Milan*', *The Hiroshima Univ. Studies Library Department*, XXXIV

(1975), 308-29, 16-18. (In Japanese with a resumé in French.)

Bb628* —, 'Sur la mobilité dans *Mobile'*, *The Hiroshima Univ. Studies Literary Department*, XXXIII (Mar. 74), 417-37, 23-4. (In Japanese with a resumé in French.)

Bb629 Tamuly, A. M., 'Un Déterminisme de comédie: A propos de *La Modification* de MB', *Australian Journal of French Studies*, IX, 1 (Jan.-Apr. 72), 86-97.

Bb630 Taubman, Robert, 'Objectivity' [MB, Romains, Vailland], *New Statesman*, LXIII, 163 (15.6.62), 871.

Terreni Azzoni, Giovanna, see Azzoni, Giovanna Terreni.

Bb631* Theis, R., 'Paris-Rom bei MB', in *Zur Sprache der "Cité" in der Dichtung*, Frankfurt-am-Main: Klostermann, 1972, pp.93-123.

Bb632 Thiébaut, Marcel, 'Le "nouveau roman"', *La Revue de Paris*, 10 (Oct. 58), 140-8.

Bb633 —, 'Les Prix' [Vailland, Mégret, MB], *Revue de Paris*, 1 (Jan. 58), 172-3.

Bb634 —, CR of Aa25, *Revue de Paris*, 8 (Aug. 58), 152.

Bb635 Thody, Philip, 'La Rectification', in J. H. Matthews, *Un Nouveau Roman?*, Paris: Minard, 1964, pp.67-73.

Bb636 Todd, Olivier, 'The New Realism in French Literature', *The Listener*, LIX, 1521 (22.5.58), 849-50.

Bb637* Togeby, Knud, 'MB', in *Der Moderne Roman i Frankrig. Analyser og synteser*, Copenhagen: Akademisk Forlag, 1970, pp. 141-51.

Bb638* Ude, Karl, 'MB über den Roman', *Welt und Wort*, XVI, 1 (Jan. 61), 31.

Bb639 Vachey, Michel, 'L'Espace indien', in Ba21, pp.91-113 (followed by a discussion, pp.114-23).

Bb640 Vadé, Yves, CR of Aa63, *Esprit*, XXXV, 364 (Oct. 67), 700-3.

Bb641 Valogne, Catherine, '*Mobile* de MB à Liège', *Les Lettres Françaises*, 946 (4.10.62), 6.

Van Laere, François, see Laere.

Bb642* Vanni, Halo, 'MB: *Répertoire II*', *Nuova Antologia* (Rome), 493 (Mar. 65), 415-20.

Van Rossum-Guyon: see Rossum-Guyon.

Van Zoest: see Zoest.

Bb643* Varela Jácome, Benito, 'La actitud intelectual de MB', in *Renovación de la novela en el siglo XX*, Barcelona: Destino, 1967, pp.407-11.

Bb644* Venaissin, G., CR of Aa20, *Combat* (27.12.56).

Bb645 Verdot, G., 'Le *Mobile* de MB va bouger sur scène', *Le Figaro Littéraire*, 844 (23.6.62), 23.

Bb646 Verrier, Jean, CR of Ba31, *La Revue des Sciences Humaines*, XXXVII, 48 (Oct.-Dec. 72), 628-30.

Bb647* Viatte, Auguste, 'Où va le nouveau roman?', *La Revue de l'Université Laval*, XVII, 1 (June 63), 899-905.

Bb648* —, 'Le Nouveau Roman', *La Revue de l'Université Laval*, 2 (Oct. 61), 122-8.

Bb649* Vier, Jacques, 'Le Cas MB', in *Littérature à l'emporte-pièce 4*, Paris: Cèdre, 1966, pp.180-2.

Bb650 Vigini, G., CR of Ab66, *Studi Francesi*, XII, 37 (Jan.-Apr. 69), 172.

Bb651 Villar, Arturo del, 'Los Narradores', *La Estafeta Literaria*, 436 (15.1.70), 253.

Bb652 Villelaur, Anne, 'Débat entre N. Sarraute, C. Simon et A. Robbe-Grillet', *Les Lettres Françaises*, 764 (12.3.59), 1, 4-5.

Bb653 —, CR of Aa12, *Les Lettres Françaises*, 808 (21.1.60), 2.

Bb654 —, CR of Aa20, *Les Lettres Françaises*, 654 (17.1.57), 3.

Bb655 —, CR of Aa41, *Les Lettres Françaises*, 919 (22.3.62), 2.

Bb656 —, CR of Aa68, *Les Lettres Françaises*, 1013 (22.1.64), 2.

Bb657* Viswanathan, Jacqueline, 'The Innocent Bystander. The Narrator's Position in Poe's *The Fall of the House of Usher*, James's *The Turn of the Screw* and MB's *L'Emploi du temps*', *Hebrew Univ. Studies in Literature* (Jerusalem), 4 (Spring 76), 27-47.

Bb658*   Vloemans, Antoon, 'Het beeld van de mens en de crisis van de roman', *De Vlaamse Gids*, XLIX (1965), 496-514.

Bb659*   Vrigny, Roger, CR of Aa20, *La Parisienne*, 42 (Mar. 57), 374-8.

Bb660   Vuarnet, Jean-Noël, CR of Aa69, *La Quinzaine Littéraire*, 47 (15.3.68), 9.

Bb661*   Vuilleumier, Jean, 'MB, l'aventure pour demain', *La Tribune de Genève* (23.9.65).

Bb662   Waelti-Walters, J. (née Walters *q.v.*), '*Passage de Milan*, le point de départ', in Ba21, pp.55-64 (followed by discussion, pp.65-9).

Bb663*   Wais, K., 'Estarrung und Bewegung. Die erzählerische Antithese Paris-Rom bei Gogol, Zola und MB', *Studi in onore di Italo Siciliano*, Florence, 1966, pp. 1179-1202.

Bb664   Waldberg, Patrick, 'Hérold ou l'enfance de l'art', *Critique*, XVI, 157 (June 60), 508-18.

Bb665   Walters, Jennifer, 'Cain and the Wandering Jew in MB's Novels', *Cithara*, X, 2 (May 71), 19-26.

Bb666*   ——, 'Gide in the Work of MB', *Proceedings of the Pacific Northwest Conference of Foreign Languages* (Oct. 69).

Bb667   ——, 'Literary Alchemy', *Diacritics*, I, 2 (Wint. 71), 7-14.

Bb668   ——, 'MB and *The Thousand and One Nights*', *Neophilologus*, LIX, 2 (Apr. 75), 213-22.

Bb669   ——, 'MB's Juxtaposed Selves', *Essays in French Literature*, 9 (Nov. 72), 80-6.

Bb670   ——, 'MB's Use of Literary Texts in *Degrés*', *Publications of the Modern Language Association of America*, LXXXVII, 2 (Mar. 73), 311-20.

Bb671*   ——, 'Notre Faust: Valéry and MB', *Western Canadian Studies in Modern Language and Literature* (Spr. 72).

Bb672   ——, 'La Recherche géographique et historique de l'identité butorienne', *Marche Romane*, XXI, 1-2 (1971), 57-63.

Bb673   ——, 'Symbolism in *Passage de Milan*', *French Review*, XLII, 2 (Dec. 68), 223-32.

Bb674   Warme, Lars G., 'Reflection and Revelation in MB's *La Modification*', *International Fiction Review*, I, 2 (July 74), 88-96.

Bb675*   Wehle, Winfried, 'Degrés: MB', in *Französischer Roman über der Gegenwart*, Berlin: Erich Schmidt, 1972, pp.57-67.

Bb676   Weightman, John, 'Art without Reality', *Observer*, 9330 (10.5.70), 30.

Bb677   ——, 'The French Neo-Realists', *The Nation*, CLXXXVIII, 17 (Apr. 59), 381-4.

Bb678   Weinstein, Arnold L., 'Eclipse: Kafka, Joyce and MB', in *Vision and Response in Modern Fiction*, Ithaca and London: Cornell Univ. Press, 1974, pp.154-214.

Bb679   ——, 'The New Novel Analyzed', *Novel*, V (1972), 274-5.

Bb680   ——, 'Order and Excess in MB's *L'Emploi du temps*', *Modern Fiction Studies*, XVI, 1 (Spr. 70), 41-55.

Bb681   Weyergans, Franz, CR of Aa42, *La Revue Nouvelle*, XXVII, 1 (Jan. 58), 99-102.

Bb682   White, John J., 'Simultaneous Condensation. MB, *L'Emploi du temps*', in *Mythology in the Modern Novel. A Study in Prefigurative Techniques*, Princeton: Univ. Press, 1971, pp.211-18.

Bb683   Whitehead, F., 'Bleston or Manchester Transformed', *Journal of the Lancashire Dialect Society*, 18 (Jan. 69), 2-4.

Bb684*   Wilhelm, Julius, 'Die *Exploration* der Stadt Bleston', in *Beiträge zur vergleichenden Literaturgeschichte. Festschrift für Kurt Wais zum 65 Geburtstag*, ed. J. Höste, Tübingen: Niemeyer, 1972, pp.389-94.

Bb685*   ——, 'MB', in *"Nouveau Roman" und "Anti-Théâtre"*, Stuttgart: Kohlhammer, 1972, pp.37-50.

Bb686*   Wilhelm, Kurt, 'MBs Romankonzeption', *Zeitschrift für Französischen Sprache und Literatur*, LXXIV, 1 (Aug. 64), 1-21; also in *Der Nouveau Roman. Ein Experiment der französischen Gegenwartsliteratur*, Berlin: Schmidt, 1969, pp.28-48.*

Bb687 Wilson, Clotilde, '*La Modification* or Variations on a Theme by Mme de Staël', *Romanic Review*, XV, 4 (Dec. 64), 278-82.

Bb688* Wintzen, René, 'Robbe-Grillets und MBs Welt an sich', *Dokumente* (Cologne), XXII (1966), 229-33.

Bb689 Witt, Susan C., 'The Equivocal Truth', *Mosaic*, VIII, 1 (Fall 74), 39-48 (followed by MB's comments, pp. 48-50).

Bb690* Wohmann, Gabriele, 'Welt in Reichweite', *Zeitwende* (Hamburg), XXXVII (1966), 125-6.

Bb691* Wolfzettel, Friedrich, 'MB', in *Französische Literatur der Gegenwart in Einzeldarstellungen* (ed. W.-Dieter Lange), Stuttgart: Kröner, 1971, pp. 402-27.

Bb692* —, CR of Ba28, *Romanistisches Jahrbuch* (Hamburg), XX (1969), 212-14.

Bb693 Wollheim, Richard, 'A Chronic Restlessness', *Listener*, 2160 (20.8.70), 248-9.

Bb694 Wurmser, André, 'MB renouvelle le réalisme' [CR of Aa42], *Les Lettres Françaises*, 699 (5.12.57), 1.

Bb695* Wyczenski, Paul, 'Vers le roman-poème', *Incidence* (May 65), 31-8.

Bb696* Yndurain, Francesco, 'Para la estética del *Nouveau Roman* [Beckett, MB, Robbe-Grillet, Sarraute], *Revista de Ideas Estéticas*, XXII, 86 (Apr.-June 64), 109-22.

Bb697* Zants, Emily, *The Aesthetics of the New Novel in France* (parts discussing MB), Boulder: Univ. of Colorado Press, 1968.

Bb698 —, CR of Ba28, *French Review*, XLIII, 3 (Feb. 70), 510-12.

Bb699 —, CR of Ba34, *French Review*, XXXIX, 5 (Apr. 66), 818-19.

Bb700 Zegel, Sylvain, 'MB et Saporta écrivent le roman-à-lire-dans-tous-les-sens', *Arts*, 859 (7.3.62), 5.

Bb701* Zeltner-Neukomm, Gerda, 'Das didaktische Gedicht', in *Das Wagnis des französischen Gegenwartsromans: die neue Weltfahrung in der Literatur*, Hamburg: Rowohlt, 1960, pp.109-20.

Bb702* ——, 'MB', in *Die Eigenmächtige Sprache*, Freiburg, 1965, pp.73-95.

Bb703* ——, 'MB', in *Im Augenblick der Gegenwart. Moderne Bauformen des französischen Romans*, Frankfurt-am-Main: Fischer, 1974, pp.90-114.

Bb704 ——, 'Von der Kunst des Zitats', *Der Monat*, 237 (June 68), 82-5.

Bb705 Zéraffa, Michel, 'Les Romanciers passent aux aveux', *Arts*, 704 (7.1.59), 4.

Bb706* ——, CR of Aa67, *Journal de Psychologie Normale et Pathologique*, 2 (Apr.-June 61), 244-5.

Bb707* Zoest, A.J.A. van, CR of Ba31, *Levende Talen* (1971), 800-1.

Bb708 Zweig, Paul, 'MB and the New Enlightenment', *The Hudson Review*, XXII, 4 (Wint. 69-70), 736-40.

Bb709 Anon., 'The Anti-Novel in France', *Times Literary Supplement*, 2972 (13.2.59), 82.

Bb710 ——, 'Les Cannibales n'aiment pas le nouveau roman', *Le Monde*, 8737 (15.2.73), 18.

Bb711* ——, 'Lettres-arts-spectacles', *Le Nouvel Observateur* (31.12. 64), 24-5.

Bb712* ——, 'MB in Bulgaria: Dichiarazioni sul Nouveau Roman alla rivista *Plamak*', *L'Europa Letteraria*, 28 (Apr. 64), 129-31.

Bb713 ——, 'The New and the Novel', *Times Literary Supplement*, 3318 (30.9.65), 847-8.

Bb714 ——, 'Œuvres en cours', *La Quinzaine Littéraire*, 13 (1.10. 66), 7.

Bb715 ——, 'Peinture à deux voies', *Le Nouvel Observateur*, 424 (23.12.72), 55.

Bb716 ——, 'The Philosophy of the New Novel', *Times Literary Supplement*, 3140 (4.5.62), 296.

Bb717 ——, 'Une Revue nommée *Degrés*', *Le Monde*, 8737 (15.2. 73), 18.

Bb718 —, CR of Aa12, *Times Literary Supplement*, 3034 (9.9.60), 575.

Bb719 —, CR of Aa16, Aa56, *TLS*, 3623 (6.8.71), 942.

Bb720 —, CR of Aa23, Aa69, *TLS*, 3450 (11.4.68), 165.

Bb721 —, CR of Aa30, Ba33, *TLS*, 3288 (4.3.65), 367.

Bb722 —, CR of Aa31, Aa51, Aa75, Ae4, *TLS*, 3592 (1.1.71), 10.

Bb723 —, CR of Aa32, Aa35, *TLS*, 3726 (3.8.73), 911.

Bb724 —, CR of Aa41, *Arts*, 861 (14.2.62), 2.

Bb725* —, CR of Aa41, *Recent French Books*, III (1962), 5-6.

Bb726 —, CR of Aa41, *Times Literary Supplement*, 3140 (4.5. 62), 297.

Bb727 —, CR of Aa54, *TLS*, 3268 (15.10.64), 931.

Bb728 —, CR of Aa63, *Le Monde [des Livres]*, 6902 (22.3.67), IV-V.

Bb729 —, CR of Aa63, Ac19, *Times Literary Supplement*, 3408 (22.6.67), 560.

Bb730 —, CR of Aa68, Ba1, *TLS*, 3262 (3.9.64), 807.

Bb731 —, CR of Aa70, *TLS*, 3767 (17.5.74), 515.

Bb732 —, CR of Aa79, *TLS*, 3342 (17.3.66), 216.

Bb733* —, CR of Ae2, *The Dubliner*, 5 (Sept.-Oct. 62), 63.

Bb734 —, CR of Ae2, *Times Literary Supplement*, 3147 (22.6. 62), 457.

Bb735 —, CR of Ae7, *TLS*, 3076 (10.2.61), 85.

Bb736 —, CR of Ae8, *New York Times Book Review* (28.12. 69), 10, 12-13.

Bb737 —, CR of Ba36, *Choice*, XI, 8 (Oct. 74), 1145.